True Ghost Stories

True Ghost Stories
Jim Harold's Campfire 4

JIM HAROLD

JIM HAROLD
MEDIA LLC

Cover design by James, GoOnWrite.com
Interior design by Jane Hagaman

Jim Harold Media LLC
jimharold.com

ISBN-10: 0989853683
ISBN-13: 978-0-9898536-8-2

10 9 8 7 6 5 4 3 2 1

Printed by CreateSpace, an Amazon.com company. Available from Amazon.com and other online stores.

DEDICATION

To Dar: The best and most multitalented person I know. Great mother, wife, professional and person. I Love You!

To Cassandra & Natalie: I am so proud! Stop growing up so fast, that's an order! Love Dad.

To Dad: Remember, they are still with you. Love you.

To Alfredo: Thanks for all you do.

To Mom & John: Love you, miss you.

To My Listeners and Readers: Thanks so much for your support. God Bless.

Contents

Part One
Ghosts and Hauntings

Part Two
Shadow People and Other Entities

Part Three
Beyond Explanation

Part Four
Pets and the Supernatural

Part Five
UFOs

Part Six
Until Our Next Campfire

ACKNOWLEDGMENTS

Thanks to my wife, Dar Harold, the love of my life, my best friend, editor, and best constructive critic.

Thanks to our Campfire callers who shared their personal stories.

Thanks Maddy, Jane and James for their help with this project.

Thanks to my Plus Club members who have allowed me to follow my dream.

Prologue
What Other Demon Friends of Yours
Should I Know About

A Note from Jim: I like to begin the Campfire books off with a story that really gets things started off with a bang. Here's one to get you in the Campfire mood. Enjoy!

This happened during the summer of 2008. I've always been a night owl, so it's not unusual that I find myself at Walmart at one or two in the morning. This was one of those nights. I didn't find what I was looking for in the store, so I got back to my car around three. I was playing with my iPod, looking for something to listen to on the way home. Then, I got this feeling that I was being watched.

I raised my head, looked around, and two or three spaces away, I saw this older, green sedan with this guy in the driver's seat. He was just staring at me. It felt like he was staring daggers right through me. Even if it wasn't paranormal in nature, it still was creepy. He was like a normal guy at first glance with shaggy, shoulder-length, black hair, and he looked kind of Hispanic. I remember thinking to myself, "Ooh, if he weren't kind of creepy, he'd be kind of cute."

Then, I looked at his eyes, and that's when my stomach dropped and I started thinking, "Oh, my God, there's something abnormal here." His eyes weren't completely black, but it looked like those theatre lenses where they make your iris look a little bit too big to be normal. Plus, they were just pure black. He was still as a statue, not blinking, just staring directly at me. I momentarily panicked, and I was recalling all of the safety training that I've ever had for single females out at night with creepy guys looking at them funny. I thought, "All right, act normal, just pull out. Go back to the street, drive to the police station, and call 911." Of course, my phone slides off the seat onto the floor somewhere, so I couldn't call 911.

I just started to head to the nearest police station, and to my dismay, I saw this man directly behind me. He was speeding up behind me, getting so close that his headlights disappeared under my trunk. I was just bracing myself for the hit, thinking that he was going to rear end me off the road, but he didn't. He was flashing his brights and honking his horn. He sped up and got next to me. He just leaned over the wheel and started staring at me. He wasn't even watching the road, but just staring directly at me.

At this point, I was practically crying. Having been goth since I was about fourteen, I was used to being stared at but never like this. This was not the stare of a normal person. I remember just feeling that whatever this being was, it was not human. I'm real sensitive to the paranormal. I've had a lot of experiences and I can sense when something is not right.

I managed to get to the street by the police station, and I was going about forty-five mph at this point. I was hoping to get pulled over by the law so this guy would be scared off. Of course, the one night I want to get pulled over there wasn't a cop in sight. I pulled into the police station parking lot, and I was rooting around manically for my phone. I didn't find it, but I looked up just in time to see whatever he was, very slowly creeping by the parking lot. To my delight, he did not try to come into the lot. Still, he was staring at me as he was driving by slowly. Then, he just disappeared behind the building.

The creepy part here is that I never saw him come out from behind the station. It is possible that he hid behind it, but I left about five minutes later, and I never saw his car come out. Then, the story gets even creepier. After I'd calmed down a bit, I didn't want to get out of my car to go in the police station, so I figured, "I'll just spend a long time in my car, I'll probably be OK."

I decided to drop by my boyfriend's house. I was in tears at this point and I told him what happened. He got this look on his face like he knew what happened. So I said, "All right, Dude, what's up? What do you know that you're not telling me?" He asked me, "Did he look kind of Hispanic with shaggy, black hair?" I said, "Yeah, how did you know that?" I hadn't even described him to him yet, and what he said freaks me out to the point that I hate to repeat it. He said, "Yeah, that was Azrael, that's the demon that I used to work with back when I was a Satanist. Since you're connected to me now, he's probably just checking you out, but probably a good thing that you came here." At least, I think that was the name of the demon or something like it.

I had no idea whatsoever that he had even been a Satanist until that moment! We had only been dating for a couple of weeks. It was kind of like, do you have any other demon friends I should know about? What else do I need to know about you? We didn't date for too much longer after that.

This was not OK, you know? I'm not a particularly religious person at all, but I know that there are things that you really just shouldn't go messing with, and this definitely fell into that category. I never saw the demon guy again, thankfully. Still, every time I'm in Walmart late at night and see a car in the parking lot with someone sitting in it, I look closely to see if it's that guy. I guess to most people it was just a creepy guy trying to chase after a girl at night, but it was just the feeling that I got off of him. I had a feeling like I was being chased by the Devil himself. Believe me, I screen my dates a lot more thoroughly now!

—*Emily, Oklahoma*

Jim Harold

INTRODUCTION TO CAMPFIRE 4

Welcome to my fourth book of TRUE GHOST STORIES—70 more stories from my popular program, *Jim Harold's Campfire*, as told to me by people from all over the world. Each of the first three *Campfire* books have hit number one at one time or another in the Supernatural category on Kindle, so book four was a natural! If you've read any of the previous *Campfire* books, thank you! If not, after you are done with this one, please check them out at http://jimharoldbooks.com.

In these pages, you'll find tales of hauntings, scary Ouija experiences, shadow people, angels, and entities that some might consider demons. Some stories defy categorization and we even add in a few UFO stories for good measure. Some tales are simple, others quite elaborate, but my belief is that they all come from a very genuine, heartfelt place.

The real world telling of these tales is what makes them very chilling, in most cases, and heartwarming in others.

The stories are edited with a gentle hand for pacing, but remain, for the most part, in the words of the original experiencer. Keeping each story in the storyteller's voice as much as possible was the first priority, so each has its own unique style and pacing. Please be aware they may not read as I would have personally written them from scratch, nor should they in my view. Hearing the real emotions and reactions of these experiencers is the fun of the book.

I hope you enjoy reading these stories as much as I have enjoyed curating them for you.

AUDIO BONUS/FREE STUFF: For those of you reading this and who have purchased my *Campfire 4* book, thank you! You can go to the "Audio Bonus/Free Stuff" page at the book's end to find an exclusive link to a bonus audio show plus other free goodies.

On this special audio *Campfire* program, exclusively created for readers of *Campfire 4*, I share and replay my five favorite stories from this compilation. You'll get to hear the original retelling by my callers. It is a paranormal countdown in the spirit of the old Top 40 radio shows. You will be able to download or stream it to the device of your choice. It is my thank you for reading the book. Enjoy *True Ghost Stories: Jim Harold's Campfire 4!*

Best regards,

Jim Harold
September 2015

PART ONE

GHOSTS AND HAUNTINGS

1

Corpse Sitting

I worked in the family business, which happens to be a funeral parlor, and I have a few stories to share.

I'll begin with a second-hand story. This was told to me by someone who had a deceased family member being tended to at the funeral home. At the departed's viewing, there were two lamps standing on a post to provide ambient light. This strangeness occurred when the person who told me the story, was at the viewing with the presiding minister standing next to him. He happened to look down at the floor and noticed that one of the lamps that was burning brightly was actually unplugged. He turned to my uncle who owns the place and said, "Your light is on, but it's not plugged in!" Well, my uncle thought very quickly on his feet and said, "It's battery operated." In truth, he fibbed a little bit so no one would be alarmed. The lamp was not battery operated in the slightest. It was a traditional plug-in, electric lamp. It should not have been burning at all being unplugged, yet it was. I'm sure if someone else had noticed that it was not plugged into the socket burning as bright as anything there may have been a small panic.

I had my own experience with this particular lamp. I was basically, for lack of a better term, the corpse sitter. So when families had to come in late and needed someone there after regular closing hours I would be there for them. Well, I had to close up one night at about nine thirty. It was dark in this building and I went into the viewing room to turn off the lights. Of course, there was the deceased there who had recently passed. I clicked off the first lamp and it went off, as expected. I went over to the other one that was by the head of the casket. I clicked the switch and nothing happened. It was still bright and completely on. I thought that was a little strange but I clicked it again. It remained on. So I said aloud, "All right, if we're going to play this game, I'll unplug it." I unplugged it. Still on. So, I looked at the deceased and I said, "You know what? Dude, I have to go home, and I can't go home until that light goes off." The light instantaneously turned off . . . by itself.

One evening, I was there by myself, other than the deceased. I was listening to my music on iTunes and I had it cranked relatively loud. On the floor above me it sounded like people were dancing and walking around. So I turned the music down and I still heard it. Then I turned it off and it stopped. It was almost like something was having fun at my expense. They were having a party and they didn't want me to be there. They didn't want to invite me. I guess I was just the DJ.

Since this is a family business, I've grown into it. I'm not licensed to physically touch the corpses and rearrange. If a family member comes to me and asks me to fix something, I have to tell them that I'll call someone who's licensed because I'm not. On the other hand, I do find it kind of creepy because as anyone knows who has lost someone, there's a big difference between when there is life in the vessel and when there isn't. You see the person and their features, but they're not there.

I have one last story. It involved a mint bowl and this is the only one that actually creeped me out. In the center of the room where I sat when I was working there was a desk. There was also a coffee table that had a little raised edge around it, about a quarter inch high so it wasn't perfectly flat. Anyhow, I was all alone again. While sitting at the desk, listening to my music on the computer I heard rattling. I looked and wondered where this noise was coming from? I noticed that on the middle of the coffee table that this giant bowl of mints was rattling and moving! That's what was making the noise. I thought how strange. I thought maybe we we're having an earthquake, but it gets a little better. This rattling bowl lifted off the table and just zoomed right across the room into the middle of the floor of the next room. There were mints everywhere and I thought, "Oh my God!" Then it dawned on me that I'd have to pick all of that up. It scared me, but I was more startled than anything.

I'm not sure what caused all of this. I would speculate that it might be the deceased being tended to within the funeral home. I can't say with certainty, because I don't know the complete history of the building.

I know historically it had been a family-owned home. There are apartments above, in fact.

My uncle lived upstairs with his wife when they first got married. So there have been a lot of people in and out of the building, and it is probably over a century old. It could be anything. Our family's funeral home has since relocated to a new building but some very strange things happened in that old place.

—Ora, Virginia

2
A Kind of Hush

Jim's Note: This story is offered respectfully for your perusal. Personally, I am a big fan of Karen Carpenter and her music so when our caller shared this story I was a bit taken aback by the coincidence. In a case like this one, I wonder about the possibility of an imposter spirit.

Regardless, what a great talent Karen Carpenter was. One sadly stilled far too soon. May she rest in peace.

I've always enjoyed the Carpenters' music. I think they're very calming and yet, groovy at the same time. This story involves Karen Carpenter and it was back when I was about twelve or thirteen years old. Karen had already passed, but they were still playing her music on the radio, so me and my siblings were familiar with them and were huge fans. One day, my brother, my friend, her little sister and I were listening to a Carpenters vinyl record album and said, "What if we have a séance and try to contact Karen Carpenter? Let's just try it and see what happens."

None of us really knew what we were doing, just what we'd seen in movies and on TV. So, we went upstairs to my friend's bedroom, sat on the mattress in a circle, and held hands. Out loud we said that we wanted to speak with Karen Carpenter, and to please use our energy and allow her to come through us. We had one of her albums playing quietly with a few candles lit. The single door into this room was closed. On the back of that door was this plastic bar that came out so you could put hangers on it. There was one hanger on this holder with no clothing on it.

We proceeded with the séance while holding hands. We said, "Come through us, do something, make something in the room move." We were all looking around the room, and I looked up at the hanger and it was slowly swaying back-and-forth. I said, "You guys, look at the hanger! Look at the hanger!" The other three all looked at the same time. My friend, who was my age, just saw the hanger moving and was a little startled. The two younger ones instantly flipped out. They jumped up off the bed and my friend's little sister fainted right there on the floor, while my little brother started running straight for the window. He was going to go jump out the window because the only way out of this room was through the door that the hanger was on, and he wanted no part of it.

I started chasing my brother, and he actually had opened the glass. He was in a panic. I caught him just in time, before he hit that window, and jerked him back. Everyone was freaking out and I said, "We have to go through the door to get out. Just run through the door, run through the door." We all did except for the girl who had fainted. We had to drag her down the stairs, but got her awakened once we got down to the living room

My friend's mother wasn't home at the time, and we felt guilty that we were doing something we probably shouldn't have been. The mom was due back in fifteen minutes, and everybody was crying and hysterical. All I saw, and all my friend saw, was just the hanger itself moving, which in itself was a fairly frightening thing. The other two seemed to really be beside themselves. Finally, we all calmed down a little bit, and I asked the girl who fainted, "Lisa, what did you see? I mean, you fainted. What did you see?" She was crying and hyperventilating, but she said, "I saw a hand. I saw a hand on the hanger and then the next thing I know, I was lying on the floor." Then, I looked at my brother and I said, "What did you see?" He said, "I saw Karen Carpenter dancing."

It gets worse. He said "Karen" was holding the hanger with one hand and she was dancing, and that was what was making the hanger sway. She was wearing like a gauzy-type flowing dress, and he said that she took her right leg and started to lift it up but it kept going straight up, like legs aren't supposed to go, beyond her shoulder. He said that's when he was going to jump through that window. He wasn't even going to open that glass, he was planning on jumping right through the window, two stories down. He wasn't going to go through that door.

It was a terrible, terrible situation. Now we were down to five minutes before the mom got home. We were all hysterical. The two younger ones refused to go back upstairs and we had lit some candles up there. We had to get those candles blown out before her mom got home. My friend and I crept up the stairs. Then and there, I experienced what might have been one of the scariest moments of my life. We came around the corner, we went into the room, and the record player was skipping. The song that was playing was *There's a Kind of Hush*. We walked into the room and we hear, *"There's a kind of hush . . . whirr . . . There's a kind of hush*

. . . There's a kind of hush . . . whirr . . ." It just kept repeating. All of the hair was standing on my body and I had chills all over. We took the needle off the record, blew out all the candles, and we were out of there.

There's actually one more tiny bit of icing on the cake of this story. A few hours later, my friend's mom said, "I'm going to take you guys out for ice cream." She had no idea we had done the séance because we would have gotten into trouble. We all got in the car, she starts it and the radio comes on. I'm not even joking about this. The Carpenters' *There's a Kind of Hush* was playing on the radio. It wasn't an eight track or a cassette. CDs didn't even exist yet. It was the radio. All of us just were like, "Oh, my God!" We asked her to change the station and we went to get our ice cream.

—*Tracy, Washington*

3

Big Dora

This story occurred about a year ago, during the summer. At the time, my daughter Isla was two-and-a-half years-old. This particular night my wife was out with her friends. It was about midnight. My little girl woke up screaming. I ran upstairs and I said, "What's wrong?" She said, "Big Dora shouted at me." I thought, 'Who's Big Dora?' After thinking on it for a bit, I figured she was talking about the cartoon character, *Dora the Explorer*.

She wouldn't take her hands off her eyes, and I tried to take them off, but she wouldn't let me. She said Big Dora kept shouting at her. So, I brought her back to my bed and we cuddled and she went back to sleep, no problem at all.

The next day my wife got back in and I told her about the night before. I went off to work and about two or three hours later, my wife called me up and said, "Isla's talking to the front door." I said, "I wonder who that is?" I listened in over the phone with my wife. Isla was talking to Big Dora at the front door. I thought it was a bit strange, but we let it go again. We thought children have imaginations so just let things happen.

Over the next two or three months, Dora became more of an obsession with Isla. It got to the point where she wouldn't walk through the house by herself, and we had to pick her up and carry her wherever she went. She would scream quite a lot that Big Dora was there and shouting at her. That made me think that I needed to do a bit of research on this. Obviously, Dora had driven Isla around the bend to bits and maybe there was something to it.

This one incident was interesting to say the least. I was sitting in the living room all alone. It was half past eleven and there was a program on the Discovery Channel about the Orient Express. There was nothing spooky in my mind at all. I was just in my own world watching it. Out of the left-hand corner of my eye, there was a shadow that walked across where the curtains were. It was in human form, but at the speed it ran, it was gone by the time I locked onto it with my eyes. Left to right it went.

That was a bit strange, but I started watching TV again. About two or three minutes later, out of the right side of my eye, right in front of the chimney breast, a figure was standing right there. It wasn't a lady, but like a twister, a tornado that was upside down. The thick part was on the floor and it went up to the ceiling. It was there long enough for me to know that there was something. It was like a mirage and it must have been there for three or four seconds. It went up into the ceiling and it gathered into a moving blob. It came from the ceiling down towards me, ducked underneath the door, and into the hallway.

I jumped up, ran upstairs, and left all the lights on. I wouldn't go back downstairs out of fright. After that, I got in contact with two mediums as Isla was becoming more frightened by Big Dora.

Jim Harold

Two weeks later, these mediums came and Isla was in the garden playing at the time. I let them in and Isla came running in the house and she said, "I can hear Big Dora!" Usually she'd say, "I can see Big Dora." This time was different.

One of the mediums crouched down to her level and said, "What does she say to you?" Isla said, "No, No, No." That gave me the chills straight away. The medium said that Dora didn't want to go and that she wouldn't talk to us. She asked Isla, "Where is Dora now?" It appeared that Big Dora had gone upstairs, so we all followed.

It turned out that the hot spot was right in front of my bedroom wardrobe. It was the usual haunting ground. Isla jumped under the duvet on my bed, and she wouldn't come out. The medium said, "Just concentrate. Just be quiet." So we stood there, the two mediums and myself, we were spread out in the room. It was freezing cold despite it being August. The two mediums were muttering away and I'm not sure what they were saying. Then, it was like someone closed a freezer door and the room warmed up. The mediums opened their eyes. They said, "She's gone. A little, fat man came and took her away." They explained to me that the reason that Big Dora was here was because Isla reminded her of her own daughter.

Since this thing had really bothered Isla, I decided to learn more about who or what was in the house. As an aside, whenever I would appear on site, Dora would run through the wall to the next door neighbors' house or she would run out the front door and down the street. Eventually I got the email that I was kind of hoping for yet almost dreading. A lady from Dover, who was a bit of a historian, sent me a photograph. It was from 1944. Our house was shelled by the Germans just before the end of the war and the information that I was dreading was in the email. There was a lady who lived next door. She died during the shelling and her name was Dora Smith. That just hit the nail on the coffin for me. It wasn't a cartoon character, but a real, deceased person. It was pretty horrendous that Dora really died so nearby and then haunted the place.

I'm not sure what to believe because things are still going on in the house. I've been told she's gone, and Isla doesn't mention her at all anymore, but bizarre occurrences continue. For example, my wife will put her purse in the kitchen and she'll go back for it five minutes later and it's not there. It's up in the bedroom. A hairbrush that was in the bathroom is found down in the sitting room without anyone having put it there. It's always ladies' things that go missing. It's never mens' items. Not long after the mediums apparently exorcised Dora, as soon as I'd leave the house all the electricity would switch off. It was at the breaker box! When I'd check, I'd find that the switch had been flicked.

Isla would always talk to the front door or go around the back of my wardrobe, because that's where Dora went. Any time I appeared, Dora would run upstairs or she would run out the door. I would often hold Isla and say, "Where's Dora?" She would say, "Dora is at the door." We would walk to the front door, look through the glass, and Isla would say, "She's outside now." We would go outside and I would ask, "Where has she gone now?" Isla would say, "She's gone next door into the next door neighbors' house." That's another thing the medium said to me. Dora wanted to bring Isla with her because she's wanted to show Isla something. Obviously, I'm not going to let a spook take my little girl away and show her something. I just found it all over the top but it was going on.

The one thing I've got 100% proof on is that Dora didn't live in this house. She lived next door, and I guess that's why she always tried to go through my wardrobe, to get into her house. My wardrobe's back wall faces her house directly next door. A two-and-a-half-year-old girl was coming out with things like there was fire and the house was broken. She'd say, "Dora's trapped she can't get out." What girl her age would say that? I had to believe Isla.

Just two nights ago, about midnight, I was watching TV. We have a dimmer switch in our sitting room, and sometimes it can fluctuate. It can be very bright and then drop just a little bit by itself. It is obviously something electrical. Two nights ago it clicked. Someone clicked it right off, totally pitch black. Dora strikes again.

Things happen here weekly but as long as they don't affect my little girl, I'm happy.

—*Steve, United Kingdom*

4

The Night Watchman

I used to work in the New York State Capitol in Albany. I began in 2007 and worked there for about four and a half years. The nexus of my story goes back to 1911. On March 29, 1911, there was a fire in the Capitol. It started just below where I worked in the library. There was one casualty in the fire, a night watchman by the name of Sam Abbott. Apparently, he was killed from smoke inhalation and tragically he was only steps away from escaping when he succumbed. It was a very, very sad thing. After the Capitol was rebuilt, just shortly after the fire, people started to see and hear things around the area where Sam died on the fourth and the fifth floors of the Capitol.

I used to work only steps away from where his body was found, and long before I was there they had some paranormal investigators come in to look around. They took your standard orb pictures and they determined the area right in front of my old office had the most paranormal activity. As somebody who's interested in these things, I decided to bring my camera to work. Starting in 2008, I started taking some pictures. I got some images of some weird orbs. They were large and bright. Since we often worked late in the legislature, I thought that might be a good time to get some shots. It was very interesting.

As I took more pictures and investigated more, I noticed in one of the images that there was what appeared to be a black figure in the hallway. I wouldn't say it was a shadow figure, but someone dressed in dark clothes. I didn't remember that person being there. I didn't hear or see anything. It was definitely a human form. When I went back to show some people, the photo had been deleted from my computer. It just disappeared, which was very strange, and I still haven't found it to this day. That only peaked my interest more. So, over the next several years I did some more investigating, and up on the fifth floor, I took some great pictures of orbs that were actually glowing. These orbs were different from the usual transparent orbs you see. They looked like lightning and they were balls of what appeared to be glowing light. Up there, I got this sense I was being watched, like there was someone there.

A few of my colleagues were working late that night, and we decided that we were going to go to the fifth floor. There was no one else around. I had my camera and we went up. All of a sudden, we got these terrible headaches, and we started to sweat and get nauseous. I said, "Hey guys, do you feel strange?" They said they did, so we decided we should take some pictures. Guess what? My digital camera didn't work. It would not work up there. It was the strangest thing. It was one of those moments that you read about and then you realize it is really happening to you.

The camera turned on but it would not take a picture. It was quite a contrast because it was working perfectly before we ascended that staircase from the fourth to the fifth floor. I said, "This can't be a coincidence." My two friends were still up there, so I said, "Let me go down to the fourth floor and see what happens." I went back down to the fourth floor, and as I got to the base of the stairs, I looked down at my camera. At the top of my vision, I saw a figure walk across the hallway, directly in front of me. I looked up and just saw the tail end of it. Again, it was a shadowy figure. By the way, my camera worked fine just as soon as I got to the fourth floor.

I called my friends and they came down, but there was nothing there. Then, we took some pictures and got these glowing orbs. Something was going on on the fifth floor. The New York Capitol is a national historic landmark, built in 1899, so it has a lot of history with a full curatorial staff. I have a relationship with some of them. Since these ghost stories are famous, I asked the curators, "What's the story with the fifth floor?" They said, "Oh, the fifth floor? That's where people have actually seen the night watchman."

Upon further investigation, I heard a story from a former colleague of mine who worked up on the fifth floor. She had just started working late one night and ran into a gentleman dressed as a night watchman. He asked her if everything was OK. She said sure and she went back to her office. In the course of her work, someone asked, "Did you see so-and-so out there, I need to ask him a question about work." She said, "No, I just saw the guard." This person asked, "What guard?" She said, "The guy. He was wearing a uniform." Her colleague said, "I don't know what you're talking about." She later saw a picture of Sam Abbott and she said that he was the man that she saw. It's really incredible.

I talked to the maintenance staff, and they told me that they've been touched as they've been emptying trash or vacuuming.

Sometimes their vacuums will shut off or somebody will whisper in their ear. Apparently, a bunch of them have asked to not be assigned to that area of the Capitol anymore. It's very, very off-putting to them. The people who give the tours tell stories of seeing a figure walking the halls on the fourth and the fifth floors. There are many other ghost stories in the Capitol, but the story of Sam Abbott is the most well-known and the one that people have the most experiences with. There's some incredible orb pictures that people have taken over the years. I know that I saw something that day on the fourth floor. I saw something walk in the hall, and what I saw in that picture was a person. It's such an old building and so much has happened. Some of that energy still has to be there.

—*Paul, New York*

Jim Harold

5
The Lady on the Stairs

I was on a night shift for social services, and I was helping this lady. Her daughter and her husband had gone away on holiday, so I had come to look after mum while they had a break, a respite. There was another daughter who had come in from Australia to help and she stayed with us.

I slept in the same room with this older woman on a cot, and she wanted to go to the toilet during the night, so I'd take her. I sat at the bottom of the stairs waiting for her. I never liked it because I always had a strange feeling there. My husband said that in the middle of the night, when you sat there, the cold air would drop down the stairs. That's how he tried to explain it away. While waiting for this lady to finish, I looked up the stairs and there was a different woman standing there.

She was large-bosomed with her arms crossed across her stomach, looking straight at me. I asked, "Is everything OK?" I had assumed this was the other daughter without her glasses on. She just looked at me and didn't say a word. I said, "Excuse me, is there a problem?" I thought that perhaps she was checking in if I was OK with her mum. She didn't answer and I said again, "Have you got a problem?" Then she turned backwards onto the stairs and went around the corner, but I could still see her breasts and pink floral nightdress.

Suddenly, the kitchen door opened behind me and it was the daughter who stayed behind standing there and she said, "Yvonne." I said, "Oh, my Lord!" I looked back at the stairs and there was nothing there. I said, "Can I speak to you when mum's been to the bathroom?"

After I took Mum to the bathroom, I came back and explained what I saw to the daughter. She said, "Did she look like me?" I said, "I thought it was you, but looking at you, she looked a lot younger." She said, "That's Mum's younger sister. Nobody's seen her, but she was so close and she got killed when she was about 37." I felt sick because it was solid, and there was nothing to say this was an apparition. It looked like a real person. I've seen a transparent ghost before and this was not that.

When I was going to go back onto duty that afternoon, I phoned the office and said, "I really don't want to go back. I didn't like the feeling on the stairs before." I said, "Could I phone the other girl, Carol, and have her do my three nights for me until I get over this?" The woman from the office said, "Carol's not going back. We were hoping that you would do all six nights, and then have one person do one night."

When I got home I phoned Carol and said, "Carol, can I ask you if you've ever seen anything at Mrs. B's?" She said, "I've never seen anything, Yvonne, but I always knew that there was something on the stairs. I'm sorry, but I can't come back. Have you seen anything?" I said, "Well, I think I have." I didn't want to make a big deal of it. I didn't want her to laugh at me. It was quite an uncanny feeling. It's lovely to hear when I hear other people tell their stories and think, "It's so similar to mine! I'm not going crazy."

—*Yvonne, United Kingdom*

6
Making Peace

For many years, my grandparents lived in what they call "The Loop" in downtown Houston. They had a separate lake house just outside of Huntsville. As time went on, they decided to purchase a more permanent residence there and relocate for retirement. They are your typical run-of-the-mill southern grandparents. They bring you chicken noodle soup when you're sick, and they are just the sweetest people ever. Their homes have always been filled with that loving, happy energy. You just always feel comfortable walking into one of their homes.

I visited this new house when they purchased it. Immediately, it was one of those places where you just walk in and think, "Oooh, this doesn't make me feel comfortable." Just one of those places where the hair stands up on the back of your neck and you are ready to just bolt out the door as soon as you walk in.

There was a lady who used to live in the house and she died of cancer. She passed away, not in the house, but in a hospice facility. Regardless, she loved that house. It was her pride and joy. You could tell that she was very meticulous in taking care of it and decorating it. She just loved it to death.

Maybe a couple of months after they moved, we found out that my grandpa actually had lung cancer. That was hard to deal with, and my grandma started to really resent living in the house. They went from being located minutes from MD Anderson, which is one of the greatest cancer centers ever, to being out in the middle of nowhere where they were thirty minutes from the nearest hospital. Grandma would say, "I hate this house. I hate living here."

She started noticing things like pictures moving around. It wasn't where you could actually see them move, but they would be in a certain spot and Grandma would wake up the next morning and they'd be in a different spot, maybe tilted or shifted to the side. Her and my grandpa lived there alone. They weren't touching them. It was just very odd. Shortly after the cancer diagnosis, they just had a lot of misfortune in the house. My grandparents aren't clumsy people, and the house was all one story. They started tripping, having a lot of accidents and hurting themselves. They were having to go back and forth out of the hospital.

One day my grandma thought, "OK, I think I know what's going on here." She's what I would call a sensitive, she can sense energy and could tell there was a presence in the house. She thought it might be the lady who had owned it previously. Grandma thought this lady was upset with her for having such ill feelings toward the house. One day while my grandpa was in the hospital and she was there alone, she walked around and talked out loud to the woman. Grandma said she felt crazy doing it.

She said, "Look, I'm sorry. I do love your house. I promise that I'm going to take care of it, and I'll do everything I can. I was just really upset when I moved in here, but I'm a good person and you can trust me." She went around to every room and said, "I'm so sorry that you passed away. I know how much you love this house and I'm going to start treating it with respect." After that it was like the veil was lifted, and the energy in the home completely changed. You now feel good when you go in there, and you're not constantly looking over your shoulder.

Plus, my grandparents stopped having such bad misfortune. My grandpa actually beat his cancer and they're doing great. I'm not saying that his cancer was linked to the house by any means. I just think that they had a lot of really bad fortune after they moved in and she started kind of cursing the house. Whatever it was, I just think that was a little more than coincidence to have everything stop after my grandma made peace with the previous owner.

It's just more of a happy place now. I don't dread going there like before. I'm actually excited to visit. It's definitely a lot nicer these days.

—*Elyse, Texas*

1

Can You Hear Me?

Before our family owned it, a man name George died in our house in the 1980s. He had a heart attack in the living room and he sat in there for about three days before his body was discovered. It is a pretty heartbreaking story because my parents had been friends with him. It was a very sad situation for them. Eventually, my family had decided to purchase the home because my mom had lived in the neighborhood her entire life.

They cleaned it up, moved in and a couple of years later, I was born. I should mention that I've always had this kind of weird way about me. I was born on Christmas so the big joke was that I was kind of different from everybody else.

When I was around the age of three, I would look over into the hallway of the house and ask, "Who are those men?" My parents would look at me and say, "What on earth are you talking about?" I still remember it today. I recall seeing these green men standing in the hallway. They would walk back and forth and would look at me. My parents thought I was weird. I remember thinking, "What the heck is going on? Why are they looking at me?" No one believed me so I just went on with life. Also, when lying in my parents' bed I would look up and tell them that I could see angels flying over the bed, whatever that means.

When my mom was pregnant with my younger brother but didn't know it yet, I sat straight up and I said to her, "A baby's coming." She said, "Excuse me? I said, "A baby's coming. Someone told me." Sure enough, a couple weeks later she learned that she was pregnant. Exactly who told me this information, I don't know. I just sat up and I said it. It was weird.

Fast forward to about two years ago, I had started to get back into the paranormal. I began looking into it because I would always hear bumps in the night around the house. I know that sounds like a generic thing to say, but I swear there was always something different about my home. This would happen in the evening. I would hear people walking around both upstairs and down. We have two cats so I just assumed it was them, until one night I realized that both of them were lying in my bed. Then, I knew something wasn't right.

On this one particular summer evening, about two years ago, I was upstairs with my mom at probably 10 or 11 p.m. It was really nice outside so we had the windows open and I was talking on the phone with a friend. We heard this banging outside. I wondered what in the world was going on. My mom asked, "Did you hear that?" We looked around, and at one point, my mom shushed me. She was so serious about it. She went to the bathroom, where you can see the back door. That's where we thought the banging was originating. I was standing in the hallway right in front of the bathroom. I swear, it still gives me goosebumps to this day, someone came up to me and asked, "Can you hear me?" It was the creepiest thing I have ever heard or experienced. I literally thought someone was behind me. I turned around and, of course, there was no one. I asked my mom if she'd said something and the answer was no. I called out to my brother Danny downstairs, and it wasn't him. No one had been there, but I felt the words and the breath on my ear. It was so strange.

It just isn't me. It seems to be communicating with my brother, too. As he's getting older, whenever he's home alone he'll hear someone saying, "Danny." It comes from upstairs, but no one is there. He's starting to hear the bumps in the night as well and it is creeping him out.

I don't know if all of this is linked to the man who died in the house. From what I've heard, he was a gentle soul. I don't feel as though there's a negative or evil force. It just feels like someone is walking around their home. I think it very well could be connected to George. As time goes on, it becomes even more mysterious. I've thought about setting up a camera or tape recorder to perform an EVP session or something, but I don't want to provoke it even more.

—*Melissa, Illinois*

8
Bunking with a Ghost

This story happened about fourteen years ago. It's my one and only ghost experience. Prior to it, I was pretty skeptical about the paranormal. It occurred on a snowboarding trip that I took with my cousin Dave and his step brother Chris. We were staying in a cabin. As we got there and entered through the garage, I had this odd feeling of being watched, like there was a presence there. I was a skeptic so I didn't pay much attention to it, but I felt it.

We ate dinner and went to bed. I took the fold out bed in the living room, Dave took the room upstairs, and Chris took the room down the hall. As I was drifting off to sleep, I heard footsteps. They started on the right side of the bed and they walked all the way around to the left side. I thought it was pretty odd. I actually sat up to see if it was a cat or a dog, and I told myself, "OK, that didn't happen." More than anything, I did this so I could go to sleep because it was a little spooky. I definitely heard

33

the footsteps, there was no doubt in my mind that I heard them, but I was lying to myself to get it out of mind.

The next morning, we got up and we went to the mountains and to do our thing. We came back and we were hanging out and talking. The lights went out and my cousin said, "Hey, come on, turn the lights back on!" The lights came back on. Then, they shut off again! After that, the guys told me, "Hey, the owners of the cabin know there's a kid's ghost in this cabin." That's when I got chills down my spine. I didn't know anything about this before, and that's when I knew those footsteps were real. I kind of freaked out a little bit, but we were packing up and leaving anyway. The guys elaborated on it as we were driving home. Apparently, sometimes the ghost locks the doors, moves things, and stuff like that.

This experience changed my way of thinking on the paranormal. Before this happened, I would hear friends say, "Well, a voice told me not to go somewhere so I didn't go and something bad happened." Before this ghost experience, when I thought I heard a voice telling me not to go somewhere, I would actually go just to tempt fate and just to kind of say there's nothing out there. After this, my perception of everything was changed.

I haven't been to that cabin since then, but I'd probably be interested in going back. It's my one and only experience, and it was as real as anything. It was something else, especially for a skeptic like myself.

—*Dan, California*

9
A Living Ghost

It was 1974 and I was having a baby. I was at the Doncaster Royal Infirmary and all the mothers-to-be were told that shortly we were going to the hospital cinema. We were going to watch a film of babies born in different positions to make us feel at ease but first we were to have a rest period. The staff pulled the curtains around me in bed and I started to doze off.

All of a sudden, there was a face in front of my mine, and I couldn't believe it. It looked like an old woman, but the features were like a man with long hair. So, I thought it was a woman. Then the person said in a broad Irish accent, "Tell Collette I can't come over, I can't move my legs." He or she, I couldn't work that out, said this twice.

Then, I rung the bell and a nurse came. I explained what had happened and she said, "We haven't got a Collette. I think you may have been dreaming." It did upset me a little bit, but I took the rest period and went to sleep. Then, we went downstairs to the cinema underneath the hospital to see the different films.

When we came back, the doctor and the nurses were at the station. They called me over and said to me, "Mrs. Chapman, can you explain to me what you've seen and how it came across?" I said the same thing, "I think it was Collette. Tell Collette I can't move my legs and I can't come over." With that they said, "We've just received a telegram, but it was for Colleen and it's the lady in the next bed and it's from Ireland and it's the grandfather. He said that he can't come over because he's got thrombosis in both legs." When she showed me the picture of the grandfather, it was exactly how I had described it to the nurse. That was unbelievable because this man wasn't dead, but he was well alive. I couldn't explain that at all. You only assume if you see an apparition, that it's a person who's died.

When she showed me the picture, it did look like a lady, but quite a masculine looking lady with very long grey hair. There's no way I could have seen this picture. I did get the name wrong as I thought it was Collette, but it was actually Colleen. Having said that, Collette was a lady who was having a baby at the same time that I had my first child, so it is possible her name stuck in my mind. I didn't know a Colleen at all.

—*Yvonne, United Kingdom*

10
Don't Be Sad

I've shared on the *Campfire* before how my mother comforted me after her death, but this additional story involved my little son. My husband had gotten me concert tickets for our anniversary. His mother had agreed to pick up our son from daycare and keep him for the night so we could go enjoy the concert. We talked about my mom a lot and still do. She's a big part of our lives. We didn't hide our grief from our son, so it was very natural that he would ask questions.

One morning, he said, "Mommy, do you miss your mommy?" I said, "Yes, yes I do." He said, "I'm going to take you in Daddy's car and I'm going to drive you to Heaven so you can see your mommy." At the time, I just thought it was so sweet. That's just a little boy loving his mommy, you know? So he spent the weekend at his memaw's, we picked him up on a Sunday morning and everything was fine.

A couple of days later when we were all in the car, my son

asked again, "Mommy, do you miss your mommy?" I said, "Yes, I miss my mommy, sweetheart." He said, "Well, she's not sick anymore and you should be happy that she feels better." I said, "What are you talking about?" I didn't want to freak him out, but I looked at my husband and I said, "Did you just hear that?" He said, "Yeah." Then my son said, "She comes in my room at night. She plays with my hair, and she tells me to tell you not to be sad because she's not sick anymore and she's happy now."

How does a three-year-old make that up, you know? I was just blown away that my son said this. It's just another way that my mom was letting me know that she's OK and everything's all right. We should just get on with our lives knowing that she's happy and watching over us.

—*Grace, Midwestern United States*

ii

She Saw Dead People, Part 1

My Aunt Mary was a very formidable woman. She was religiously very devout, but no stranger to spirits and such. She just had a very calm and accepting outlook on the matter and she passed it onto others in my family, including me.

I have several great stories about her. One was about a friend she had whose husband had passed and the strangeness that ensued. This happened right around the beginning of World War II. My aunt had family in Germany, and she would always go back and forth to visit them to make sure they were doing well. Of course, her trips were interrupted during the war.

Her friend's late husband was from Germany and he had wanted to be buried back in the old country. My aunt was going to take his ashes back, but she couldn't do it because of the travel restrictions. Ever since he had died, his spirit was very restless.

He would just walk up and down the stairs every night. My aunt said you would regularly hear disembodied footsteps going up and down her friend's stairs and it was driving this widow crazy.

Finally, my aunt was able to go to Germany, and they had a handmade box in which this man's ashes were going to be carried and laid to rest. However, they'd never actually thought to put the can of ashes into the box until my aunt was getting ready to leave and the can didn't fit. As you can imagine, at this point the widow lost it. She became hysterical and began crying, "He's never going to rest. I'll be hearing him walking up and down the stairs for the rest of my life!"

My aunt was a woman of action and so she said, "Get me a can opener." She literally opened a can of green beans, put his ashes into the smaller can, put the can in the box, and sealed it up. She took it back to Germany and my aunt said, "He never walked anymore." When she shared this story with us as kids, we were more impressed with the fact that she'd seen human ashes! We didn't even care about the fact that there was a spirit running up and down the stairs.

—*Jean, New York*

12

She Saw Dead People, Part 2

The story I told you earlier about my aunt Mary and her run in with a friend's ashes was great, but I have one that I think is even better. It's my all-time favorite story that she told us.

She was a private nurse for many years, and she worked for both the very poorest and wealthiest people. On this occasion, she was working for a very well-to-do family that had a summer home and she traveled with them. I believe this was in the 1940s when everything was very structured and formal.

This particular evening, after the children were tucked in, they decided to have a séance. My aunt was in the room as the people at this little party sat around the table and started. My aunt looked up and saw a man in a white shirt, a tie and pants standing there, but the strange thing was that he had no face. It was blank! For whatever reason, she found that hysterically funny and she started laughing. Of course, it caught everyone in the room by surprise. They were asking her, "What are you laughing at?" She said, "There's a man standing there and he has no face. He's obviously not a good person. He's embarrassed to show his face."

If that wasn't weird enough, then he went through the wall to the room where the kids were sleeping, and all of a sudden, they started screaming that someone was pinching them. The blank-faced ghost apparently woke them up, pinched them and, understandably, they became hysterical. Everyone went to calm them down. After they got everything settled, these people started the séance again. My aunt broke into laughter this time, as well, and the kids started screaming that they were being pinched again!

She said she couldn't help from laughing because the whole thing just tickled her funny bone for whatever reason. At that point, everyone decided that enough was enough. I never knew why they had the séance in the first place. I don't know if there was something there and they were trying to figure it out or if it was simply for fun like someone today might play with a Ouija board. Again, when she told us kids about it, we were kind of nonplussed because we expected it from her, but my aunt really was something else.

Occasionally, she'd say, "I couldn't sleep last night. I had a parade of people going past my bed." We'd hear these things, and never even think twice about it. One time she asked me to go hang a picture back on her wall that had fallen. The nail on which it was hung was about six inches long and bent all the way up against the wall. The only way that picture was going to fall was if it were lifted up and off the nail. I asked, "Where did you find this picture?" She pointed to the middle of the floor. It was a hand-made drawing. She couldn't remember who had drawn it, and I said, "I think he passed and this is his way of saying good-bye." She agreed that it was very possible.

She never pooh-poohed it if you said you'd heard or saw something otherworldly. She said, "Oh, it's nothing. They won't hurt you." She was a very religious woman. In the 1940s, she had a near death experience in a dentist's chair. Nobody talked about stuff like this then and she actually saw the gates, Heaven, a garden and beautiful lights. She was told she had to go back and she was very upset because she didn't want to return. Eventually, she did. The dentist was flipping out, slapping and shaking her to revive her. She was one of a kind. It's unfortunate you don't fully appreciate someone like that until you're much older.

—Jean, New York

13
Ghostly Treasure

This story about my grandma was handed down in our family. It's the reason I believe in ghosts. She was a devoutly religious Mexican woman and, while I didn't hear it directly from her, I know if she told it to others it was true.

In 1945, she was living in Mexico with my grandpa where they were renting a home from her uncle. She was seven months pregnant at the time. They had just moved into the house and one night she woke up and she saw a shadowy outline of a man at the foot of her bed. Of course, this scared her witless. She said a few prayers, pulled the covers over her head and it disappeared.

A few nights later, the same thing happened again, except this time the spirit called her by name. She didn't know what to do and was freaked out. The spirit went on to say that he wanted my grandma's help. Once again, she pulled the covers over her head and it disappeared.

Something about it terrified her and I can't blame her, seeing that she was pregnant at the time. It struck her so severely that she convinced my grandpa to move elsewhere because the second time was just too much for her.

So they moved, but it didn't work. The spirit came back again and this time he explained to her that he wanted her to help him with some spiritual debts that he hadn't taken care of during his lifetime. Specifically, he wanted her to light candles in a nearby church and give thanks to God on his behalf.

Apparently, he had hidden some money in the front yard of her uncle's house. My grandparents weren't living there anymore, but the spirit told her that if she dug beneath a tree there that she would find twelve clay dolls surrounding a clay pot. In that pot she would find some gold coins. The spirit said she was to use the money to perform the spiritual errands he'd requested.

Something about this last interaction calmed her fears. The spirit said, "Don't be afraid as I just want to help you. I want this money that's left over afterward to be for your baby." He also mentioned that her child was going to be a girl.

My grandma told my grandfather about this. So, they went back to her uncle's house and they started digging. They didn't ask permission. They just started to dig. Someone told her uncle, explaining why there were digging, and he came home to put a stop to it. He told them, "No, you can't do that. You're crazy. This is nonsense. You can't be digging here."

So, they left and you can guess what happened. The uncle dug in the spot and he found the dolls and the money, just as the spirit said. He opened up a store with the money he had found. Everything the spirit said came true. My grandma did end up having a baby girl, and she wasn't able to help the spirit exactly as she been instructed because her uncle spent the money. However, she did light some candles in the hopes of assisting the spirit.

The store her uncle opened with the spirit's money failed. You have to wonder if it was doomed from the beginning because of how the money was used against the spirit's wishes.

This is such a classic ghost story to me that it almost sounds like something from a movie and that intrigues me. My grandma had thirteen kids. She was very no-nonsense and this story was out of character so I believe it completely. She wouldn't have benefitted from it, and she didn't tell any other stories like it. For a story like this to have been told by her is fascinating to me.

—*Marty, Oregon*

14
Haunted Housesitting

A round 1990, my then-boyfriend and I were about to move from Illinois to Washington, and we were in between places for a few weeks. My sister lived in Illinois, as well, and had gone on vacation. She asked us to house sit and watch her dog, which was perfect given our situation.

Going in, I knew she had had a bunch of strange things that had happened in that house. I don't remember if I told my boyfriend beforehand. The house was fairly new for that era. It was built in the fifties or sixties. So, it wasn't like a big old spooky house. It had brand new, white carpet and everything was pristine.

The strangeness ensued on the first evening while we were sitting at the little breakfast bar that was in the kitchen. We were eating and all of a sudden, we heard voices. My first thought was that someone's alarm was going off at the wrong time. You know, sometimes set your alarm for 6:00 p.m. instead of 6:00 a.m.? So we went searching through the house to find a clock radio to turn off but we couldn't find one. Everywhere we went, the voices never got louder or softer. They stayed exactly the same and we both were hearing them. We walked around and finally we went upstairs to where the bedrooms were. No radio was on, nothing was on. We went back downstairs. Finally, it stopped. Boom, it was done. We thought it was strange, but we wrote it off. Then, I remember telling my boyfriend that my sister had weird experiences in the house.

Later that evening, we went into the screened-in porch area where the TV was. It was an addition to the house and connected to the living room by a sliding glass door. This was late August or early September and it was still hot out. My sister wouldn't allow smoking in the house, but we both smoked and she said it was fine if we wanted to have a cigarette on this porch. So, we went out there to watch TV and we partially closed the sliding glass door that led back into the house. We left it open about two inches because we knew my sister was going to call that night from Florida, and we wanted to hear the phone.

We were watching TV and I said, "I want some Cheetos." My boyfriend got up to get them and the door was closed shut. Not partially shut as we left it, but completely closed. The funny thing was that I was sitting right in front of it on the floor, the door was about three feet away, and I did not see it close. That's what always freaks me out about it, I did not see this happen.

Anyhow, the door had a patio security bar. You know how people have a sliding glass door and to protect yourself you put in a long bar to secure the door? They had one of those, and when we went into the room, we moved that bar about two feet away from the door. We just left it there on the floor. We were not on a hill, we were on flat land. It is Illinois after all, so it should have stayed put.

So, he went to open the door, and not only was it shut, but

it was secured by this bar from the other side! We were locked into this porch. We did not see this happen, and didn't even have a spooky feeling. I don't know how that bar could have rolled two feet and set itself perfectly in place, but it did. My boyfriend had to exit the porch to the outside and find the spare key hidden elsewhere on the property. Then, he let himself in the front door and let me out of that room. We just thought that was very freaky.

Several nights later, my sister returned. We were still staying there, but at this point we were in the basement. It was not spooky. Quite to the contrary, it was completely decked out with a game room and that kind of stuff. It was nighttime and I was sleeping on the couch while my boyfriend gallantly slept on the floor. Suddenly, I woke up with the feeling that someone was staring at me.

I should mention that this house was built over an old Indian cave in between a cemetery and a golf course. I think that comes into play here. My boyfriend started talking in his sleep, and he began repeating something very strange over and over. He kept saying, "You know, there's a lot of empty graves over there in that graveyard. There's a lot of empty graves over there in that graveyard." He scared me so badly, that I stepped off the couch and almost stomped on his head.

I woke him up and I asked him to stop. He had no memory of saying it. I felt like something was communicating that there were empty graves, that there was something there that we didn't know about. That's what was going through my head.

I didn't feel it was personal, not like they were beckoning us to the graveyard. I felt like they were telling us something. My sister's thirteen-year-old boy had seen a floating head in his bedroom over the TV that looked like Mark Twain. He said he got scared when he saw it, of course, but then he kind of leaned up. He sat up from his bed and squinted to see it more clearly. Then, he said the head did the same thing back to him! The head came forward and squinted back at him.

Anyway, we never got a clear answer about what was around that property. Cemetery, Indian cave, who knows, a bunch of weird stories that don't fit together. I don't know of anything else strange like that happening in the house since then. As far as I know, the house is still owned by my sister's in-laws, but they're in their 80s and not the sort of people that would ever talk about such things. The guy is not my boyfriend anymore, but we're still very close friends and we share a really freaky story.

—Amy, Washington

15

Uncle Fred Is Still Here

When I was about twelve years old, my Uncle Fred passed away. Shortly afterward, we had some very strange goings on that lasted for years. My uncle had a bunch of old furniture including an old fashioned rolltop desk, a really heavy one. Well, my mom brought that home plus a few other things of his, and maybe she brought back more than she realized.

At that time, I had the habit of reading in bed before going to sleep. I would read late into the night because it took me a while to fall asleep. One night when this all started, I had finished reading and turned off my light. I shut my eyes, but I kept hearing this noise in the living room that sounded kind of like a brass knocker handle. We lived in an apartment and it was just me, my mom and our two cats. I was in my room with one of the cats, and my mom was sleeping in her room with the other cat. I thought about it and figured I was just hearing things, so I shut my eyes again.

A few moments later, I heard that knocker sound again. I immediately thought there was somebody in the house. Mind you, I was twelve at the time, so I was quite scared. I reached into my nightstand and I got out my scissors. I crept out of my room, and I was turning on every light in all the rooms as I went through the hall into the den, just to make sure no one was there. I went into the kitchen and switched out my scissors for a big butcher's knife. I was really scared that somebody was in the house.

I went into the living room where the rolltop desk was. Keep in mind, my mom is an immaculate person. Every time she does something, she makes sure she closes everything up and puts everything where it's supposed to be. My mother wasn't even sitting at the rolltop desk that day. Yet, the rolltop desk sliding mechanism was pushed up and both of the top drawers were open and pulled completely out. Not to mention that they had brass knocker handles! The desk came with a swivel chair, and instead of it being pushed in under the desk like it usually was, it was positioned as if somebody had pushed it back, turned and gotten up. I just thought it was very weird. I didn't think of my uncle, really, until many years later.

In the meantime, I was growing up. I was becoming a teenager and bringing boys home, even though they were mainly just friends. Uncle Fred didn't like the guys that I would bring home. I had a friend who had stayed over one night, and he was sleeping on the couch in the living room. The next morning, he had told me that he had an experience where he was paralyzed and he couldn't move. He couldn't hardly breathe and he heard somebody whispering his name in his ear but there was nobody there. Before he went to take a shower, he had all his stuff in his duffel bag except towels. We let him use ours since he was staying with us for a little while. He took a shower, and when he came out, he couldn't find the towels that were hanging on the rack. He looked all over the place. Turns out they were folded up nice and neat . . . in his duffle bag. Just weird little things like that would happen.

The next major thing that happened was when my fiancé/soon-to-be husband was living with us. I was ill at the time, so I slept in my bedroom while he slept in the living room. He chose to sleep on the floor. He had a big quilt for a cushion, sheet, and a couple of pillows. In the middle of the night, he went to the bathroom. He came back to find the sheets and quilt folded up completely perfectly. They were piled on top of the pillows, just sitting in the middle of the living room floor, as if someone was trying to send him a message to leave.

It was a protective spirit. That's why I thought it might be my uncle, because I never felt threatened. I never had the feeling like somebody was watching me. There were no creepy feelings or anything like that. It even played with my cat. It was the weirdest thing. One day I remember clearly there was a spider on the ceiling, and my cat was sitting on the coffee table meowing at the ceiling, but the spider was behind him. The cat was playing with something, getting up on its hind legs, meowing and pawing at absolutely nothing. He was looking at the ceiling and meowing, and yet the spider was behind him. He wasn't paying attention to it, but something else that was up there. It was the strangest thing.

I'll be forty-two years old at the end of this year, but Uncle Fred followed me and the activity continued for much of my 20s. When we moved I had had a baby and little strange things would happen. In our last apartment in New York, Colorforms, you know those vinyl cutouts of cartoon characters, they would end up stuck to the very highest portion of the window. These were very tall windows that went all the way up to the ceiling. There was no way Colorforms could be put up there by me, much less by my little three-year-old boy. So, really weird things kept happening.

One night, just before we moved out of New York, I had a dream. In it, I was in the old apartment where I grew up. Specifically, I was in my very first childhood bedroom, only I was an adult and Uncle Fred was there. We were standing in my bedroom talking. At this point, all I remember him saying was, "I've been with you for the last thirteen years but now I have to go." Then I woke up, and I thought, "How long has it been?" So, I called my mom and I said, "Mom, when did Uncle Fred die?" She gave me the date and the year and I calculated it. It had been 13 years just like my uncle said in the dream.

It was a positive experience and I wish he would come back. I do. I really wish Uncle Fred would come back.

—*Lorraine, Tennessee*

16
Historical Ghosts

few years back, I worked at the Greene County Historical Society in Waynesburg, Pennsylvania. The building was formerly a poor farm started in the 1800s when every county was required to have one.

The very first day I was there, while sitting and learning about my work, I heard disembodied footsteps walking around. I wondered what was going on. So, I checked out the place. The building is pretty large. It is a fifty-two-room museum, so I walked around and looked outside first. There were no cars around, and there was no one around inside or out to generate these footsteps. After walking around for a bit and not finding anything, I went back to work.

A few days later I was chatting with someone there about this, and he said, "Oh, just wait to see what happens." A couple of weeks later, I was working down in the library which is separate from the museum. I was making prints. I felt like there was something in there with me, and I got the impression that it was like a guy in a green army outfit. It was very weird and it was so distinctive. I went back up to the museum itself, and I caught one of the interns who used to work down in the library. I asked, "Hey, when you worked down there, was there anything weird that went on?" He said, "Are you talking about the soldier in the green outfit?" I was blown away. I couldn't believe that he and I saw the same thing. We never spoke about it before, but yet we had the same experience and that's not all. When it was published in the local paper that we'd had this experience, someone came to the museum, about a week and a half later, and said that her neighbor had seen the same soldier there. I was pleased because it gave me validation, and I knew I wasn't crazy.

These historical objects, especially when we'd touch them to create exhibits, felt like they had a soul. It is kind of weird, but you feel like you have a connection with these things. I think that's what could have been at play here.

The history of the place made it all the more intriguing. Sometimes you'll go to a museum that is newly constructed for millions of dollars and they put these items in it but it is not the same. The whole structure where I worked was a part of the history itself. I believe it held people's souls. Over 150 years of life existed here being a poor farm and then a museum. A lot of people have been through that structure over the years.

I think it is also important to remember that these people were not happy. I actually found some papers that there were reports of abuse of the residents before the state got involved in 1949. There was actually a dungeon, and it held the insane. They were called inmates because they were wards of the state. They were beaten, and sometimes even killed by their caregivers.

It's a sad place and you can feel that. When you walked in on certain days, you felt the air was so thick that you knew something might happen. There were so many things that went on there. The other day I talked to one man, who happens to be a paranormal researcher, and he believes that there's a shape-shifter running through a particular hallway in the museum, which has a dollhouse on display. He said that to him it looks like a fat bullet with boomerang shaped wings that looks like a machine and flies like an airplane.

We have a harvest festival every year and have for decades. One year this couple was talking to a vendor, and a lady walked up in period clothing, and was conversing with them. They had an enjoyable conversation, and then she walked away. They asked the vendor, "Who was that lady?" and he said, "What lady?"

We created an event around this phenomena. We had a lot of people come out, but leading up to the event we had so many things happen. It was held in a barn we have on the property, and a couple of days before, one of our workers walked in there and saw this little boy, about three-years-old. The boy had blonde hair and was wearing a dress. He said the little boy looked up, smiled, walked away, and disappeared into thin air. We knew right then that this was more activity picking up. It was like these spirits knew something was going on soon that would impact them.

I spoke with a woman who was a Harvest Festival vendor in the cobbler room, which was the first room down in the dungeon. As she was working there, a lady walked in with a vintage nurses' uniform. This nurse was pushing an elderly man in a wheelchair, and she looked up at the vendor and said, "Oh, excuse me." She turned around and disappeared just like the little boy. Many people involved in the event had strange experiences, even a preacher who came out to help. I recently left there, but I'll always remember it.

I'll always have a fondness for the paranormal. When I was about ten years old, I had an experience where I saw a mysterious farmer. He walked across the street and through the grass, right in front of me, and disappeared before my eyes. He was completely out of his element and didn't even notice me. He was wearing dirty overalls with a red bandanna in his back pocket. He was chewing on wheat and had a pitchfork over his shoulder. He didn't even look like he was from our time. Ever since that first experience, I've had a love for the supernatural.

—*Larry, Pennsylvania*

Jim Harold

17

Our Little Girl Ghost

In 2008, our military family was stationed in southern Japan, and we decided that we wanted to live in a Japanese home versus one on base. So, we decided to move into a home that was built in the early 2000s. It was a newer home. When we first moved in, we would hear footsteps, like those of a little kid running, and we just thought the houses are built really close together here in Japan. The walls were not very well insulated, so we just thought it was our neighbor kids.

My little girl at the time was just two and I was pregnant with my second. We really just thought it was the kids next door, but I would get so spooked sometimes I would actually go sit outside. The summer after we moved in, my friend, who lived about a block from us, started having some strange things happen at her house too. I was there one night and I heard someone say, "Mommy." It wasn't just me who heard it, there was my friend and six other people in the house who heard it as well. We thought it was one of our children, so we looked, but they weren't even anywhere near where we heard the voice.

Fast forward about a year, or year and half ahead. We were still hearing the footsteps. One night, I had a dream that we had three girls. By this time, our second daughter had been born. I woke up the next morning, went to my girl's room, and I was confused because there weren't three girls in there, there were just two. I was so confused that I went to my husband and I said, "Where's our other little girl?" He said, "We don't have another."

It was very real and very vivid. The little girl in the dream was the same age as my older daughter. At about that time, my daughter started telling us about a dream she kept having, about a little girl who would come visit her in her room and they would play. I assumed since I'd been listening to my older daughter talk about this girl, I was dreaming about her too.

One day, my husband called for my older daughter and she didn't come. He looked up and thought he saw her standing and coloring at her little chalkboard. He said, "Honey, why aren't you paying attention to me?" She completely ignored him. He looked at her and the chalkboard, and then looked at my youngest daughter who was sitting on the floor playing. Then, to his surprise my oldest daughter walked out of the living room to the left. It hadn't been her coloring on the chalkboard at all.

My husband, is a sailor through and through, very level headed and very analytical. He said he was just stunned by what he saw next. He said he just went and sat down, he was so stunned. He said there was another little girl standing there with dark hair, just like our daughter. She was the same height but she wasn't one of our girls.

It all revolved around our oldest daughter, mostly. She was four-and-a-half or five at the time. A week later, I sent my older daughter upstairs to get something out of her bedroom, and she was taking her sweet time and I hollered up there, I said, "Come on, let's go." I heard footsteps coming from the bedroom to the top of the steps, they came down the steps, and then I didn't hear anything. I figured my daughter had stepped off the hardwood floor onto the carpet where you enter the living room. I said, "Come on, babe, let's go." Nothing happened. Then, she walked out of the bathroom, which was on the other side of the house. I said, "Where were you?" She said, "I didn't go upstairs yet, Mommy."

Another night, we were sitting at dinner and I looked up and there was somebody walking down our hallway, child height. My girls were with me and so were my friend's little boys. All the children were present and accounted for, except for our ghost girl.

Right before we moved back to the States, I was talking to my mom about this ghost girl. She said, "Please don't bring her home with you." I was going to be moving in with my parents. I said, "Mom, I'll do my best to make sure she stays in Japan." After we left, my friend who had been having odd experiences called me and said, "I think your little girl is at my house." I said, "What do you mean?" She has two little boys so she kind of welcomed the extra girl in the house. She said that the boys' toys had started disappearing. They have one of the little hand-held game systems and she put it on top of the TV where the boys couldn't reach it. She went back to get it and it wasn't there. She asked her husband where it was, and he said, "I have no idea what you're talking about." She found it a week later in her hamper upstairs. Stuff like that happens all the time to her now, so maybe our girl has found another home.

I have no idea who this girl could have been. We were in

southern Japan, and we visited some of the different sites there. My friend has a theory that something followed us home. Why not? I had two girls! What's one more?

—*Kelly, Tennessee*

18
Dad's Crossing Over

This was in May 2012. My dad had been ill for something around eighteen years. He had a type of dementia that we think may have been alcohol-induced. For the last several years, he had been in a nursing home in Arkansas. He had been going to the brink of death and then bouncing back for a few months. So, we all kind of knew his death was imminent. I was not able to get out there to see him, but I talked to him on the phone a couple times. He remembered me as his daughter but as a baby. In retrospect, they were funny conversations.

This one evening I dreamed that I was in my hometown where my dad raised me. We were at the river. There is truly a river in this town. We were standing on the bank and he was with me. I didn't see him, but I knew he was with me. He said, "You have to help me. I have to cross, I want you to come with me." I said, "No!" It was immediate in the dream, I was like, "No, I can't. No! I'm not going with you!" The last thing I heard, was him suddenly saying, "My liver was an alcoholic." I woke up just like that.

I woke up from this dream and looked at the clock. It was 1:48 a.m., which was Pacific Time. I started to think about the dream for two seconds, and I thought, "OK, I think that was Dad." Boom, my phone rang and it was my sister calling from Kansas. She said, "I just got the call. Dad died. He died at 3:39 a.m." Which was 3:39 a.m. Central Time, which would have been 1:39 a.m. Pacific. Literally, within ten minutes of his death, I had a dream where my Dad said, "I have to cross, I want you to come with me." I said, "No." It is the second time in my life when a loved one had come to me when they passed. It is amazing.

—*Amy, Washington*

19

The Doctor Is In Again

My mom was in a nursing home for rehabilitation after she had her knee replaced. My husband, four friends and I came to visit her one night after work. We decided to sit at the end of this hallway that didn't have any patients so we wouldn't disturb anyone with our loud conversation and laughter.

At the time, my mom was seated next to a fire extinguisher cabinet. It was a big cabinet with a mirror. We were all visiting and laughing. My husband was seated across from me and I was on a couch. I noticed that whenever I talked he wouldn't look at me. I thought, "Jeez, is he mad at me about something?" That didn't make sense because everything was fine before we sat down in the hallway. It was weird because I tend to be kind of loud while telling funny stories, and he just wouldn't look at me. I thought, "Oh, brother, here we go." I thought I was in trouble.

We visited for a few hours, and then we left the nursing home. When we got outside I asked Keith, my husband, if he was OK since he seemed rather standoffish towards me during our visit. He was kind of shaky and he said, "You won't believe what happened to me in there." He said that a man appeared, standing right in front of where I was seated on the couch, looking directly at me. I freaked out and insisted that he tell me everything before we started driving. This figure was a tall man with white hair, and he had a long coat on like you would have seen in the 1920s or the 1930s. He was holding a large satchel, and he was standing there looking down at me. He didn't move at all, and right before the man appeared, my husband felt as though someone walked behind him. Keith looked over his shoulder and there wasn't anyone there but when he looked forward the man was standing there, just staring at me.

We assumed he was a doctor because a few weeks ago we watched *American Pickers* where they buy old collectibles, and they had bought an old medical bag. That's when we realized what the satchel was. Keith said that was the exact same type of bag as this man was holding, so he must have been a doctor.

Later, after we told my mother what happened, she mentioned that she thought she saw someone walk by that evening, but that was impossible because there was absolutely no one there but us.

I tried to do research on it to see how old the nursing home was, and it was from the 1960s. I haven't yet been able to find out what was there before the nursing home, because I think I would have to go to the county and rummage through the records. I haven't taken it to that extreme yet.

Again, he had on the old kind of long coats that they wore and he had white hair. I don't know if he had glasses on, because Keith could only see the back of his head. He said that it was freaky that he was a tall man, and he was just standing there looking down at where I was sitting. I've never seen a ghost, so I don't know if it was a residual haunting. Keith said he could see the man completely, but he was transparent, like an apparition, but a see-through kind. He just stood there, he didn't move at all.

My husband said that he'd never go back down that hallway again, and you know, he's not a baby. He's from England and he even had a ghost in his flat, so he's seen things before but for some reason this completely freaked him out.

Maybe it was an older doctor who used to be a part of the staff there, I don't know. Perhaps it was something like a spiritual recording of sorts replaying. I don't know what it was, but it did freak us out because he was staring at me, even if he didn't mean anybody any harm. You don't expect to encounter something like that when you go to visit your loved ones.

—Janet, Illinois

20

A Painted Lady

Halloween happens to be one of my favorite holidays and let me tell you why. My husband and I bought a house in 2004. It's a Painted Lady Victorian from 1892, and we purchased it towards the end of June. After moving in, we noticed some strange things going on, and this continued until about the beginning of November of that year.

Most of the activity happened upstairs on the second story. We used to have the den up there set up with a television, a love seat and a sofa. This is where the first of the incidents occurred. We had been there about a month at the time and I was watching TV. All of a sudden, I had this whiff of a very strong perfumed powder, like women used to wear generations ago. I don't own any perfume because my husband gets a headache from it, so I have nothing like that at all in the house. It was so overwhelming that it kind of stopped you where you were at in your tracks. I was trying to figure out where that smell was coming from. It just kind of wafted up out of nowhere. We thought that was kind of odd.

That happened a couple of times, and then we would hear footsteps right above us in the attic. Now, the only way you could get into the attic is if you have a ladder, and on top of that there's some drywall that you have to move out of the way. When we went up there we found that it had all been spray-foamed by the previous owner. So, hearing boots walk on wood just wouldn't make sense, but we'd still hear footsteps that sounded like boots walking on wood. It was very strange.

All of this kind of built up over a period of several months. The next thing I can remember was one bright, early afternoon when I was starting to walk down the stairs. As I was descending, clear as day, I saw this orb about the size of a golf ball come up the stairs and then shoot out the outside wall. It kind of had a white outline with a more translucent light in the center. It just shot out of the wall to the outside. I thought that was even more weird because it was daylight and that it was an orb. I wasn't expecting that.

A couple of weeks later my cat had a moment out of a horror movie. She was sitting on the steps and staring into space which in and of itself is not unusual for a cat. Then, all of a sudden, her head started to move rapidly back and forth. Extremely so, not just a little bit. Her head went completely to one side, and then completely to the other at such a rapid pace that it looked like something out of *The Exorcist*. It was as though she was looking at something that was moving so quickly back and forth in front of her that she didn't want to lose sight of it. It really kind of freaked me out because I had never seen her head move back and forth that quickly. It lasted about thirty seconds, and then she lost interest in whatever it was or it disappeared. I didn't see a thing. I just saw her rapidly moving her head back and forth, and it never happened again.

The final culmination is this one big event. As I said, it was around the beginning of November. It was nighttime and my husband was already asleep. I was trying to, as well, but the air felt very thick, and I just couldn't get to sleep. I kept tossing and turning. Plus, I kept hearing what sounded like footsteps out in the hallway.

There's a different weight distribution on the floor when an animal walks versus when a person walks. This sounded like a person, not an animal. Being in the heart of the city this was disturbing because you naturally might assume the worst, a break-in of some type. I was just lying there and listening. All of a sudden, out of nowhere on the side of the bed in my right ear, I heard a woman's voice whisper, "Can you hear me?" Just like that, "Can you hear me?" I stayed still, looked up and stared at the ceiling. I didn't react because I'd never had a ghost speak to me before. I just pretended I couldn't hear it, but I could, and it was clear as day. It was a person whispering into my ear. There was no way to misinterpret it. When it asked, "Can you hear me?" The emphasis was on the word "hear." I thought that was interesting.

Somehow, I actually managed to sleep that night, but the next day I told my husband what had happened. Of course, he jokingly said to me, "Well, as long as she doesn't tell you to kill me we're OK." For some reason that day, I just kind of pulled the name Annie out of the air, and I started referring to the ghost as Annie. I was compelled to do some research on this house, and I found out that the people that lived in the house the longest were a Mr. Saunders and his wife . . . Annie! Needless to say, I got the chills when I learned this. It really freaked me out. I had just started calling her Annie for no reason, or so I thought. I don't know where I picked up that name. After that incident, the paranormal activity calmed down. Occasionally, I would still get the perfume powder smell that would just waft up out of nowhere, but that was pretty much all that happened from then on. Maybe once Annie was acknowledged she was satisfied?

—*Micki, Colorado*

Jim Harold

21

Roses Were Her Favorite Flower

had a great aunt named Bert who was my grandmother's sister. She was one of three sisters. These were cool old ladies from a Lithuanian immigrant family. Anyway, I didn't know my Aunt Bert all that well, but I knew her through family and evidently we made some kind of connection though we weren't extremely close. Aunt Bert was very unique.

The last time I saw her was at my grandmother's funeral. My grandmother was the first of the three sisters to pass on and I flew in from Washington to Illinois to be with the family. I went straight from the airport to the funeral home, and as I walked in my Great Aunt Bert was sitting there in a wheelchair. She was dressed in white and she had that light white old lady hair. She was already in her nineties at this point and she was just glowing. I walked up to her and I said, "You know, you look so beautiful, you're just glowing. You look like an angel." It seemed to take her a few minutes to figure out who I was. Finally, she looked at me with recognition, patted my hand and said, "Thank you, I needed that so much." That really endeared her to me. I didn't really know her, but at that moment I realized despite all the austerity she really had feelings.

That was the last time I saw her. About four years later, she died. I did not fly home for that funeral, because I didn't have the money. It didn't seem that pressing. I knew she had died, but I was kind of OK with it. I knew she was ninety-eight-years-old at that point, she had a long life, and had traveled a lot which she loved. She was a funny woman and she had a great philosophy in life that got passed through our family. Not necessarily followed, but passed on, where she said, "I never argue. If I'm wrong, I can't afford to and if I'm right I don't have to." That's how I remember her and it's a great philosophy. I kind of felt good. I thought, she loved to travel and she was on her next adventure.

My boyfriend and I had just broken up. We were still living together in separate rooms because we didn't have the finances to go out on our own yet. My ex-boyfriend had kindly given me twenty-four roses in a vase, a huge glass thing that we used to actually put change in. He had cleaned it out, put some roses with eucalyptus in there, and gave me a book that I had wanted. He did it in recognition that we were going through a breakup, my great aunt had just died, and a bunch of other things were going on that were very hard at the time. He just kind of set them out on the table as a little acknowledgment.

Within a week of Aunt Bert's death, I was sitting alone in my house. The roses were there in the vase. My Aunt had died, my boyfriend was gone, and it was a sunny afternoon in late autumn. In Seattle, it's rare that it's sunny so I remember it well. My cats were with me, but they were all asleep on the water heater in my kitchen and I was writing in my journal. All of a sudden, there was the most extreme presence behind me and I was terrified, absolutely terrified. I couldn't move and I wouldn't look up from what I'd just written. The saying about the hairs on your neck going up? It's not just a saying. They do and they did.

I heard something. It was a very light *swish, swish, swish* kind of sound to my right, and I was afraid of it because when I looked up I knew what I was going to see. I finally brought myself to look up and the flowers were moving. There was no breeze in the house as I have no windows in that room. There was no heat in that house except for a wood stove in a different room. It was not lit, so there was no blowing heat, no doors open, nothing. These flowers were not blowing side-to-side. They were moving up and down in the vase kind as if they were being arranged or being picked up by invisible hands to be smelled. It was as though you saw someone standing there lifting, shifting, and moving them around and smelling them! That's what they were doing. I saw this in the bright light of day and I was literally paralyzed, staring at it and asking, "What do I do now?" I looked at the cats and they were still sleeping. I was hoping that they would been freaked out in order to give me some validation, but they were out. No proof there so I got up and went into the other room because I was really freaking out. I was really, really afraid. I couldn't understand why the flowers were moving!

Suddenly, this thought came into my head, "It's Aunt Bert." I don't know where the thought came from, but it just came and my body got really, really calm. I thought, "Oh, I'm sorry." I felt really embarrassed that I had been frightened by my aunt.

Two days later, I spoke with my nephew, who lives in Illinois, and he had gone to my Aunt Bert's funeral. He was telling me who was there and so forth. As I was talking with him, I realized the day the roses were moved was the same day Aunt Bert was buried! I decided to tell him what happened to me and he said, "Amy, it was on the program at the funeral. Roses were her favorite flower." Then, I realized what happened was definitely true. It was her and she just stopped by for some reason. That made me happy.

Maybe she felt I needed a little reassurance, but I bet she probably felt badly that she scared the crap out of me before I realized what was going on! I think it was real. I really do.

—*Amy, Washington*

22

A Frightened Little Ghost

I was living in my first apartment ever in San Francisco, and I was just falling asleep.

I think it was probably ten minutes after drifting off when I felt this brush on my face. It was like a hand was touching my face. I opened my eyes and there was the glowing face of what looked like an eight-year-old boy. It was pretty terrifying. I jumped back in my bed and back against the wall since my bed was against the back window. Then, the boy started to transport to the foot of my bed, but it wasn't really like he walked. It was like he appeared at the end.

I was just freaking out. I was totally paralyzed and I couldn't move. The lamp was by my left arm and I couldn't move my hand because I was just so scared. He was standing there and I could only see his torso. He was wearing this newsboy cap and there were green-yellow-blue neon lights. They were all moving throughout his body. It wasn't like the lights were there, but they were just sort of streaming light. It was going down his torso and down below his legs.

At that point, I didn't even know what was going on. Was I dreaming? I didn't know. I picked up enough courage to turn on the light. Right before I reached to turn it on, he appeared at the end where my door was and where I hung my coats. His head was looking down, sort of like he was ashamed. I turned on the light and he was gone. The whole thing lasted probably a good 30 seconds.

He didn't say anything while he was there, but like others who have called your program, I felt I knew what he was thinking. He didn't mean me any harm and he wasn't a bad or evil entity. It was someone who was trying to tell me something. I felt his innocence and his age. Maybe something had happened in that building, but he wanted to tell me something. I think he felt that I was scared. When I pushed against the back wall, he got scared and then he put his head down in shame.

I feel like there was something frightening, but I have no idea what he was trying to tell me.

The building was older and it was right by San Francisco State University. I feel like the building was rebuilt maybe in the 1950s, but it could have been older. Maybe it was something that was there before. Either way, it was frightening.

—Mary, Canada

23

Molly

I work in a local hospital in the supply department. It's sort of an old hospital built in the early to-mid 1960s. The supply department is in a building that used to be an old church. Two weeks after I started working there, I found out that where I work was not only the supply area for the church but also where bodies would be prepared for church funerals.

Right after I started, I was hanging out in the department with a couple of coworkers who had recently gotten new iPhones. They were playing around with the camera app. They were taking pictures and they snapped a picture of one of my buddies, who was sitting at a computer in the department. Also, there was this huge big brown door that always closes on its own that was in the picture as well.

In the picture this door was propped open. There's no way it could have done that because as I said, this door just slams itself shut. Not only that, but there was a white shape in the doorway that looked like a girl in 1800s Victorian-era looking clothing. My buddy showed me the picture, but I really didn't think too much of it at the time.

Later on that day, I was by myself there and I was stocking because I was going to be delivering supplies to the OR. Everyone else was either delivering or already on lunch. I was putting some catheters into my basket and I looked out of the corner of my eye when I saw this black shape. I wondered, "What was that?" I looked and nothing was there, so I went back to putting stuff away. I looked out of the corner of my eye and I saw it again. It stayed there. It was this three or four foot little girl dressed all in black with long black hair.

I froze, then I blinked and it was gone. What's kind of crazy is that I told everybody about this later that day, because obviously I freaked out. My friend, who was in that picture with the little girl, told me, "Oh yeah, the people upstairs in accounting, they have a name for that little girl. Her name is Molly." Accounting is located on the floor above us and it turns out she's there all the time. They'll see chairs moving and hear tapping on the keyboards.

One woman was working at two or three in the morning and she saw someone walking through the accounting area on the security cameras. Everything was locked up tight from the outside, so she wondered how in the world someone had gotten into the department. Security came, they unlocked everything, looked, and they said, "This thing's been locked and there's no way anything could have got in here." Regardless, this woman swore she saw something. So there's all kinds of weird stuff going on.

I've gotten used to it since I like this kind of stuff and because it's not really like a poltergeist. It's not like a demon, but it's just a little girl. It's not a very malevolent presence. What is actually kind of ironic is that I only submitted my story to the *Campfire* a few days ago, but I've actually had something happen to me again last night that involves your show.

I went into work kind of early yesterday which I do quite a bit to beat the traffic. A buddy of mine had a Halloween party the night before and I said, "Oh screw it, I'll just go to work straight from his party." I got to work at one in the morning. What was more ironic was that I was sitting there listening to *Campfire* on my iPod, just staring off into space and killing time. I started hearing footsteps running back and forth above me from the accounting department. I thought it was weird because I was listening to your stories and I was hearing something. I figured it was nothing, but then it started getting louder.

At first, I thought it was something going on in my iPod maybe on your program, so I paused it and took my earbuds out. I could still hear the running upstairs. I said to myself, "No, I'm not doing this." So I locked up and I went to Denny's. I wasn't staying at work any longer!

—Zack, California

24

You See Her, Too

I am an estate liquidator so I've seen some strange things in the course of my work. In this particular case a woman, I'll call her Dottie (not her real name), had passed away and she hadn't been gone very long. Her only child, a daughter, hired me and my sister who is my business partner to help clear her home out. I came to find out that Dottie had been agoraphobic, and she did not leave her house often. Her home was her palace and she loved it. You could tell. She had decorated for years and had a gorgeous yard.

This house was designed in such a way that you could go from one room to the next in a complete circle. It had an open floor plan. You could go from the dining room, to the kitchen, down the hall to the bedroom, through the living room, and end up back in the dining room. You could see everything. So, we started working. I'd be standing at the sink typically washing things and I'd see my sister, or so I thought, coming out of the hallway into the den. I would turn to see if she needed me for something and nobody was there. It happened every time and I kept thinking that maybe I was just seeing furniture out of the corner of my eye.

Soon, my sister and I had moved a lot of furniture out of the den to create a flow for people when they came in. We moved things around, but I kept seeing something out of the corner of my eye! Well, it happened again and this time I decided not to turn and look, but to keep observing from the corner of my eye. It was a woman who didn't look like my sister. She got about halfway to the den and I was so scared by that time, that I caved in and turned to look. No one was there.

Unbeknownst to me, my sister had been experiencing the same thing and she thought it was me. She'd be in the bedroom working, hear "me" come to the door, turn around and no one was there. Then, she started seeing a woman going from the dining room into the kitchen, as I had as well.

We really didn't say much to each other about it. The next door neighbor would come over every evening after it got dark. She would bring in the mail and turn on a couple of lights to make it look like someone was home. In the morning, she would return to turn the lights in the house off. We had met her since she was helping the family out.

So one day my sister and I were in the living room, taking a break, and I was facing the wall. Suddenly, I saw a full-figure apparition by the door. I was so scared I put my hands to my eyes, and my sister didn't know why I was so freaked out. At the end of the living room where the hallway turns around, in walked the neighbor lady. All three of us screamed. The neighbor had come in from the garage to tell us something. Well, when we told her why we were so scared she said, "You've been seeing her too?" We said, "Yeah, what have you seen?" She said, "I quit coming over here after dark because I keep seeing Dottie going from the dining room into the kitchen."

Me and my sister started recounting what we'd been feeling and seeing. The neighbor said, "I'm not coming back over here anymore, with what you've all been seeing. Dottie was my friend, but it just scares me too bad."

Not only did both of us and the neighbor experience this, so did Dottie's son-in-law. The daughter and her husband lived just a couple streets over and we became friends with them both. He'd come over and check on us. Sometimes, he'd make us go out to lunch. One time, we called him to say that there was a box of personal stuff that we'd found, the type of stuff you wouldn't sell, that he needed to come get it and that we were going to go out to eat. He said, "Fine, I'll swing by and pick 'em up, and then meet you there."

When he got to the restaurant, he looked funny and he had always been a really jovial, happy, jokester kind of guy. I thought something was wrong and he said, "Girls, I'm going to tell you something. You might think I'm crazy, but I went in there to get that box and I swear I was going to bump nose to nose with my mother-in-law." He said, "She was so thick in there that I barely grabbed the box and ran. Now, I loved this woman like a mother, but it just scared the poo out of me." We had verification and we hadn't told him a thing. I would never tell a family something like this. It would probably upset them.

—*Torey, Texas*

25

Ghost Workers

I work in a facility in Ohio that used to be a manufacturing plant for a large vacuum corporation. There are multiple companies there. The company I work for does manufacturing there and we have got a big section of the place. One Saturday morning, I went in and I was there by myself as the person on the previous shift had left. I went out to my job area and I was walking about 50 yards when I heard somebody walking beside me. I looked and there was nobody there. I started walking again and I heard the footsteps again. I stopped and then those footsteps took off, like somebody just ran away from me.

I was getting squirrelly. I was hearing little conversations going on, and I couldn't place them. I figured it must be in one of the other plants in the building. The strangest thing that happened was once when I was walking back to my office. I was going down the aisle and at the corner up there was an intersection ahead of me. There was an office that had windows on three sides and I looked through two of them at an angle to the oncoming aisle that I was walking toward. I saw a guy walking toward me like he was going to meet me at the corner. He looked at me and smiled. He had blond hair, a striped shirt, and I wondered, "Who's this?" I had never seen him there. I got to the corner and there was nobody there.

The place is massive and I think it has history clear back to the 1800s, if I remember correctly. It even had its own coal plant, infirmary, and it was a self-contained community. After the large vacuum company left, my company was the one that took it over.

I haven't verified anything yet, but I'm going to be doing some research. The most recent experience I had was when I was on the phone walking through an abandoned section of the plant. The production area is separate from the main office area. I was walking through the abandoned part talking to my mother on my cell phone. I had lost signal and I said, "Mom, can you hear me?" The line was dead. I heard garbled stuff, but it wasn't her so I just hung up. I got a call a couple hours later from my mom saying, "How long did you hold the phone?" I said, "Once you said such-and-such, I hung up." She said, "The line held for another two minutes and at one point I heard somebody saying, 'I'm here, I'm here. Come get me, I'm here.'"

There have been tons of stories that have come from this, because I talk to my co-workers and ask, "Are you guys seeing this? Is this real?" I have so many stories. One guy hears whistling. He'll be in the plant alone at night and he'll hear somebody whistling to the point that it will aggravate him. He'll tell them to shut up and it stops for about two minutes. Then, it chimes up even louder in his ear. There is more to the strange, old place than vacuums.

—*Neil, Ohio*

26

Did You Hear What I Heard

I have three daughters, an eight-year-old and a pair of four-year-old twins. When my oldest daughter was around three or so, we had quite a scenario play out. On this particular evening, we had done the bedtime routine and put her down for the night. I was in the bedroom at the other end of the house and listening in on the baby monitor.

My wife was with my daughter and I heard them talking on the monitor. My wife was discussing grandparents and she was explaining about how her mother was our daughter's grandmother and my mother was her other grandmother. Then, they got to my father who died in 2000 before my daughter was born. He never met his granddaughters and vice versa. They were talking about it and my wife mentioned my father and said, "Well, you've never met him." My daughter pointed to the corner of her room over her closet and said, "Yeah, I see him. He comes up, comes up right there and sees me sometimes." I was hearing all this over the monitor and thinking, "Oh, my goodness!"

My daughter went onto say, "But he only pops his head out at night." I went out into the hallway and my wife stuck her head out of the door and said, "Did you just hear what I just heard?" I said, "Yeah, I did. That was kind of unexpected." So our daughter went to bed and she was fine. A couple of days later, she informed us that her grandfather had popped his head out again to tell her that he loved her. That was the first incident and quite striking.

For the second story, I need to backtrack just a little. We actually had a fourth daughter who was delivered stillborn, and we had named her McKenzie. My wife was driving in the van with all three of our girls and they were talking about my wife's boss' daughter, who had been over to play. She's the same age as my oldest daughter, and they were discussing her. Her name is Kelsey. So one of our twins, Brianna, said, "I can't wait to play with McKenzie again." My oldest daughter and my wife were like, "You mean Kelsey, right? Her name is Kelsey." Brianna was insistent. "No, McKenzie. I mean McKenzie. I want to play with her again." They said, "You're sure? You mean Kelsey, right? The little girl with blonde hair who was over here playing?" Brianna said, "No, I want to play with McKenzie. She's got long brown hair and she plays with me at the house." She was insistent that she was playing with her sister McKenzie, as far as we can tell.

—*Clair, Maine*

27

A Mother's Presence

My story started back in 2009 about two days before Christmas. My mother-in-law was from New Orleans and she had driven up here to Georgia with her boyfriend to spend Christmas with us. It became a holiday we'd never forget but not for a good reason. My mother-in-law arrived, stepped onto my back porch and collapsed as she was talking with my husband.

I was trying to get home from work and there was really bad traffic with a bunch of wrecks. When I pulled up to our house, there were ambulances, sirens, and lights. I thought surely they were there for another house. When I got out of my car and ran up to my front door, it was standing wide open. It turned out that my mother-in-law had a massive heart attack and she passed at the young age of fifty-two. It all happened right on my back porch.

My father was an EMT for many, many years and he was at our home when this happened. The bizarre thing was that he had her breathing but she died after she was passed over to the local EMTs. I don't know exactly what happened.

It was a shocking experience. Instead of preparing for the big holiday, we were getting ready for a funeral just two days before Christmas. We sent her body back to New Orleans for burial and went down for the funeral. That's when strange things started happening. The first was when my husband's grandmother told me that she had seen my mother-in-law in her kitchen the day of the funeral. She said that she looked just like a normal person and that she had been making coffee.

She also said that two days prior to the death of my mother-in-law, that she saw my husband's father, who had passed over twenty years earlier. Just like my mother-in-law, he was in the kitchen making coffee too! That was really strange.

Things started to get a little bit weird around my house, as well. After we finished the funeral and went home, small things started happening. Little things around the house would start to move or disappear. Keys, remote controls, cell phone chargers . . . little things like that. Then, they'd turn up in weird places. We'd find them on a kitchen table when they had been left in a laptop bag. I'm in the technology business, so I'm always carrying around a lot of little strange pieces. I try to keep them together and in my laptop bag so I'm always ready to run out the door. When things like that started moving and disappearing, I figured either I was losing my mind, or my husband was playing jokes on me.

My husband is a nurse, so he works a lot of weird hours and I'm always coming and going out of town. Our schedules are both really strange, so sometimes I would be home alone all night. He wouldn't come home until seven or eight in the morning. I started to hear talking while he was gone. It sounded like two people having a conversation outside and that was really bizarre. When he's working and I'm in town, I usually house clean in the middle of the night. This way, I get to spend all the time I have with my husband. One night, I was cleaning and I heard somebody sitting down on our old couch in my bedroom. It's a really distinct sound because that piece is about 250-years-old and the wood creaks. You can really tell when somebody sits on it.

I started hearing that a lot and it began to happen while I was sleeping. I'd be in the bed and I'd hear the couch creak next to me like something was sitting there. My husband sleeps like the dead, so he wouldn't hear it. I got in the habit of bringing my cat in the room with me. I know that sounds silly, but cats are really sensitive to this kind of thing. She would sleep at the foot of the bed and any time she would hear that creaking noise, her ears would prick up. She would walk up onto me and poke me. I would sit up and look around and see the cat. She would get this really crazy look on her face and run out of the room.

About three or four weeks after all of that concluded, I had to go back on the road. I went down to Corpus Christi, Texas to work a job. In the middle of the night at the hotel room, I had literally the covers completely ripped off of me. I was sleeping and the covers went flying. This was a new hotel so it was really weird. My job has taken me all over the world and I've stayed in tons of hotels in many countries. I'd never bumped into a haunted hotel, so I was really freaked out. Of course, the thought of an intruder runs through your mind. The covers came completely off of me and there was nobody there. I stood up, looked around the room, out in the hallway and there was nobody there. I turned on all the lights in the hotel room, went back to bed and somehow returned to sleep.

Then, I had a dream about my mother-in-law. In the dream, I could see her and she was talking to me. She was telling me what she wanted me to do with her various properties and things like that. She told me how she wanted me to raise the children that she thinks I'm eventually going to have with my husband. It was as though we were communicating, even though she had passed on.

I finally woke up and I called my husband. I said, "You're never going to believe this, but I just had this dream about your mother." He said, "Well, I heard her talking out on the porch today." He went outside and there was nobody there. He was in Atlanta, so it was very bizarre. This sounds really bad, but at that point I was starting to get kind of freaked out.

Finally, I decided that when I got home, I would pour holy water across both of the doorstops and I would say a prayer. I would smudge the house and tell my mother-in-law that she was welcome. I would ask her politely not to disturb things. I'm fine with somebody communicating with me in dreams, but when things start moving it makes me nervous.

I should tell you that after I said the prayer and smudged the house, a lot of the activity calmed down. I still hear people talking outside and still have occasional dreams, but there's nothing being moved and there's nothing crazy happening anymore. It has calmed to a level that's livable.

I think the reason this happened is this: my husband is from a very strict Catholic background, and my family is Baptist. My mother-in-law and I never really had the time before she passed to talk about some of those issues fully. She was a very strong lady and a very dominant personality in life. I think that part of the reason is because she died so suddenly, that she feels the need to pass her viewpoints onto me even after death. I think that that is what is sparking the communication and what has kind of continued this whole dialogue.

Jim Harold

We're definitely trying to keep her memory alive and to make sure that we do her justice. This year on the back porch I have Christmas lights out there. I had a nice candlelight vigil and told her that it was for her. I wanted to make her feel welcome and tell her that she's still part of the family.

—*Melissa, Georgia*

28
Footsteps

I came from a blended family. Between my dad, my stepmom, and six kids we needed more space. Just like all the classic horror movies start off, they found this great big house at a really ridiculously low price.

It had been abandoned for three years, so following the script we moved right in! Sometimes you'd feel like you weren't alone and there was kind of an oppressive feeling in the house, but all in all it was just kind of spooky. The most active thing was that every night there were the sounds of footsteps on the staircase.

They would start on the landing, come up to the second floor, and then start on the landing again. This was such a regular occurrence that, after a while, we just didn't pay any attention to it. It was just something that just happened.

One late summer night, when I was thirteen or fourteen it was very warm. We didn't have any air conditioning, so we had all the windows and doors open. We used box fans. I was lying in bed and the whole house was dark. Everybody else had gone to bed and these footsteps were coming up the landing again.

At first, I didn't really think much of it, but this time was different. All of a sudden, I heard something go into my brothers' room. I wondered, "What was that?" It had my attention at this point. I looked out into the little hallway there and this apparition of a woman came gliding back out into the little hallway. Her hair was piled up into this bun and she had this high-necked blouse on with long sleeves. She had a long skirt, but she didn't have any feet! She was just kind of floating there. I didn't see the bottom of her skirt, her feet or anything. She looked at me and I looked at her. I wasn't freaked out, just trying to figure out if this was real. Was this happening?

She looked at me and I looked back at her. She looked away, and she glided back down the stairs. That's the biggest thing that's ever happened to me there, I thought that was dramatic enough.

—Grace, *Midwestern United States*

29

I Know, He Told Me

I have two daughters. My oldest was from my first marriage and when she was about five-years-old, I was pregnant with my second child. I had told my first daughter that I was having a baby.

Later on, I found out it was going to be a girl. So, one day I went into my daughter's bedroom to tell her that she was going to be having a little sister. She said, "I know!" She pointed to the corner of her room, right above her window, and she said, "He told me I was going to have a little sister." She held her hands out like maybe about ten inches apart, showing me the size. I looked up to see if there was anybody there, but I didn't see anyone. It was weird the way she said it. She was really happy about it. I really didn't question her too much. I believed her.

At first, I thought it was an angel or God or something, but I really don't know. I accepted it and said, "OK." It was kind of strange.

—*Lily, Florida*

30

Grandma's Perfume

I'll tell you about my grandmother. I come from a very religious background, so I have a tendency to chalk us a lot of life experiences as "God things." The first one that I can really recall like that was with my grandmother, my dad's mom. In 1994, I lived in Oklahoma and she was in Illinois where my parents lived. I was in my late twenties and like many people that age I was pretty self-absorbed. I wasn't paying much attention to the rest of the world. It was all about me back then.

My parents called to tell me that my grandmother was very ill and that they were taking her to the hospital. I was pretty lackadaisical about it and said, "OK, I'll go up there at Christmas and see her and spend a little extra time and everything will be fine." The next phone call I got from them was to tell me that she had passed away. I hadn't taken the time to call her, tell her I loved her, and ask her how she was feeling. I hadn't done anything. It was a very immature part of my life, and I pretty much beat myself up with horrible guilt over it.

I went to stay with my family in Illinois for the funeral. My mom and dad were sleeping in my grandmother's bedroom, my brother and sister-in-law were sleeping in the guest bedroom, and I was out on the sleeper sofa watching late night TV. My grandmother wore one perfume, and that's all she ever wore. It was called *White Shoulders* perfume. I was there watching TV, and it wasn't just the scent of *White Shoulders* that came through the room, but it was like a wall of it. The smell was incredibly thick, moving from one side of the room to the other side, and I immediately sat up and said, "Grandma?" I had shed quite a few tears over the whole guilt thing with not calling her and everything. I took it as Grandma giving me the opportunity to say what I needed to say. So, I poured my heart out. I told her that I loved her and that I was sorry that I hadn't called. I felt so much better, and then the scent just sort of moved on. Then, I went to sleep. The funeral was the next day. I stayed in that house two weeks afterward, going through her things and donating stuff. I was there completely by myself and it never happened again. It was just that one night. Like I said, I chalk things up to "God things" sometimes and to me, that was God letting me have my one last time with my grandmother.

I felt like a tremendous weight had been lifted off my shoulders. I felt like I had connected with her, she heard what I had to say, and that it was all OK.

—*Julie, Oklahoma*

31

We Used to Live Here

This goes back to when I was about eleven or twelve-years-old. I'm twenty-three now, so it's been a while. Every week my family would have gatherings where we would just have dinner and hang out with other family members. On this special night, we were all together at an aunt's house and one of my uncles had just arrived. He had to use the restroom, and as he walked down the hallway, he saw a bunch of little kids playing around. He didn't recognize them, they weren't part of the family, and he assumed that they were the neighbor's children.

Then, he walked into the restroom, and as soon as he shut the door, there was wild pounding on the door. He asked himself, "Who would pound on the door when they just saw me walk in?" So he opened the door, looked outside, and no one was there. The kids that were playing there were gone. So, he turned around and closed the door. He later told us that he saw a girl sitting on the toilet with her hair down. He automatically assumed that it was

105

just a person sitting there, so he turned off the lights and walked out. As soon as he walked out, he figured the girl would say something since he shut off the lights. She didn't, so he came back to the table, sat down, and didn't say anything at the time.

Later on in the night, my grandma's brother and sister were sitting there, just having a normal conversation. My grandma's brother seemed like he was shooing somebody off of him. He kept saying, "Get off of me, get off of me. Go play somewhere else." My grandma's sister said, "What are you doing?" He said, "Look at this kid right here. The kid keeps jumping on me. He keeps trying to play with me, and I'm trying to tell him to go play somewhere else." She gave him a really weird look because there was nobody there.

Seeing all these little weird things happen, the family started talking about it. After the festivities were over, everybody went home. My aunt who owned the house went to bed as normal, but that night in her dreams all these kids came to her. These kids came to her in her dreams and told her, "Oh, this is our house. We used to live here. We died here." She woke up and that was it. Weird little things happened and no one got into detail with it, but that was probably the most major thing that happened there.

It is a weird story and I was there, but I don't really remember it because I was so young.

—*Jonathan, California*

Jim Harold

32

A Friend's Weird House

My friend lived in a very strange house. One of his roommates and his girlfriend made a suicide pact and killed themselves in the kitchen of the house. That was just the beginning. Next, my friend had another roommate drop dead on the front yard while mowing. My friend came home and found him lying there. The house looks unassuming but has this sinister backstory. I had my own strange experience over there a year or two after the suicides.

My friend and I were in a band together and we had shot a video. Three of us were watching the recording at his house. Suddenly, we heard a bang, like a crash coming from another room. My friend got up, went out to investigate, and the window at the end of the hall had blown out and was laying on the floor. The glass was not broken like you'd expect, but the whole window assembly was laying, intact, four to five feet away from window frame. He picked the thing up and jammed it back into the frame.

There were two by fours around the window and it was maybe a two foot square window. I went behind him and tried to pull the thing back out, and it was so snug that I would have really had to wrench on it to pull it out. He just shrugged the whole thing off. He said, "Yeah, that kind of stuff happens here at this house, all the time." We occasionally get windstorms up here and they can be pretty extreme, but there was no wind that night, and I can't imagine a rogue gust coming along strong enough to blow that out.

It would seem with that kind of power, whatever it was would have actually blown the glass out. I don't understand how the glass was not broken. The whole window fixture literally flew across what is essentially a hallway. So, it was pretty bizarre. There were three of us there and the other two of us were pretty freaked out. My friend who lived there seemed resigned to it, very matter of fact about the whole thing.

There are some other stories surrounding that place that I didn't witness personally. For example, my buddy and a friend were hanging out watching a movie or something. They stepped outside to smoke a cigarette and when they returned inside minutes later, they got a real surprise. A collection of stuffed animals, teddy bears and such, that were all on a curio cabinet had all been turned upside down. They stepped outside to smoke a cigarette, stepped back in, and all these stuffed animals had been placed upside down with nobody else in the house.

That window flying out like that was an interesting experience. It's the only thing I've ever personally witnessed that really made me wonder if there really is something to the paranormal.

—*Ben, Washington*

33

Growing Up in a Haunted House

I don't live there anymore, but I grew up in a haunted house. It was about thirty minutes west of Chicago in Elgin, Illinois. There were just so many strange things that happened to my family. I lived with my mother and my older sister in that house. We had a little dog, as well. I'll tell you about just a couple of stories.

This happened on a hot and steamy August afternoon. I like big band and swing music. I was listening to a Glenn Miller song in my room and I was humming the tune. All of a sudden, I heard in my ear very, very clearly, "Great tune, isn't it?" I shot down the stairwell and I went down like every sixth step, running to my mom who was in the kitchen. She said, "You look like you saw a ghost." I said, "No, I didn't see one, but I heard one."

The house is about 100-years-old and is still standing. It was built on an old graveyard which dated to about the 1830s. I think that house was so haunted because they had moved the bodies buried there in the 1890s. They just dug everyone up and threw all the remains into large carts and relocated them.

They had all these new building projects of homes and that was the priority, not the people buried there. I later found out that the house that I grew up in was in the center of that cemetery. There were tombstones and bits of mausoleums just all ground up in the dirt in our back yard. Weird things would happen and it didn't really matter if it was at night or in the day.

Another story was when I was in the finished basement and on the computer. I was typing away and noticed someone standing behind me. My sister had already moved out and my mom wasn't home at the time. The basement wasn't very big and I would know if an actual person was down there and there wasn't. Still, it looked like someone was standing behind me. I looked down to see someone's shoe and a pant leg there. The pant leg was to a late 1930s/1940s style suit. It was pinstriped and had a cuff at the bottom of the pants. The leather shoe was very shiny and it made an indentation in the carpet. When I looked behind me, no one was there. Nothing in the carpet, but it was clear as day I saw the shiny shoe in the monitor of my computer screen.

I later found out that a gentleman named Mr. Halper had died in the house in the early 1950s. I kind of thought that maybe that was him. There were several times when I was by myself in the house listening to my music loudly. All of a sudden, it would be like there was this rush of energy coming to my door and it would feel like it wanted me to turn down the music. I always thought that was Mr. Halper.

I used to shut my bedroom door when I went to bed because otherwise it would swing open by itself. The doorknob would just rattle and rattle. The first time it happened I think I probably turned purple, I was terrified. After six years of living there, I barely noticed the last time it happened. I used to lock the door with an old skeleton key to keep it shut. I'd unlock the door, open it, and no one would be there.

It seemed that ghostly happenings would pick up around Christmas. When the air got dry and static electricity got going, it would come in waves. There would be months that nothing would happen and then they would start up. It would cycle back and forth like that but it would always happen around Christmas time.

One time, when I was alone in the house I went downstairs to get a glass of water in the kitchen. I had to walk through the living room, and when I did, I felt like I had walked naked into a room or something. It was as though people were looking at me and it seemed very still. It was like I wasn't invited. I quickly said, "I'm just going to get some water." I did and I ran upstairs. I felt like these "people" were quite annoyed with me walking through there.

I moved from the house since then, and I don't know if people still experience things in that house. I guess they do because everyone in that town, especially in my neighborhood, have weird things going on. We all have almost like pet ghosts. I don't know if it's because of that cemetery, or if it's because Elgin is on a ley line, the magnetic lines stretching across the world.

We were kind of going through some tough family stuff at the time. I've talked to my mom about it and she said that we just really should have left. It was just a negative place to be. At the time, we just kind of thought it was normal. Things would disappear and reappear. Mom would always see full body apparitions and strange things. I think some of it was time-related. It was like a time-slip, kind of flowing through or bleeding in. Others,

I think, were spirits or some type of energy from the people who were disturbed from their eternal rest. I think it has something to do a mixture of time, energy and space. I think each is key to what was going on in that house.

—*Kirby, Illinois*

PART TWO

SHADOW PEOPLE AND OTHER ENTITIES

34
Shadowy Spider

I was around eighteen years old when this happened. I'm over forty now, but I will never forget it. Back then you didn't hear about anything like this and you sure didn't talk about it. My boyfriend, now my husband, used to work, no pun intended, the graveyard shift. Before he would go to work he would nap for a couple of hours, so I would go over to his apartment and cook him dinner. Then, he would lie down for a little bit. I would clean up, and sometimes I'd lie down with him until he'd fall asleep and then I'd get up and leave.

This was on Waverly Street. It was one of those type of apartments where a lot of people would get single rooms and they'd have a common bathroom. His place was on the second floor. I've had a lot of creepy experiences throughout my lifetime, but never ever anything like this before. Going up the hallway to his apartment, I was creeped out, like I was being watched but I never understood why. It really felt like someone was watching me. I took a shower there before and I just felt like I had to get out. It was creepy.

On the one occasion, I can remember lying down next to him, and he was lying to my left. The bed was against the wall and I was lying on the edge of the bed, facing a little black and white TV that he had to the right of me. I fell asleep and I remember in my dream it was complete blackness. I felt a heaviness on my chest and I thought I was going wake up, but when I felt I had woken up it was just into another shade of blackness. It was like I woke up from a dream just to go into another a dream. I was terrified.

Usually, I realize I am dreaming and I can control them but not this time. I was wondering why I couldn't wake up. Maybe a week or two later, the same scenario happened. I fell asleep to this little six-inch TV, that was the only thing lighting up the room. This time I had the feeling I woke up, but my body was completely paralyzed, and I thought to myself, "Why can't I wake up? This is so awful, why can't I wake up? I can't move." All I could move were my eyes, but that wasn't the scariest part. I had this fear, this dread, like I was being watched. It still creeps me out to this day. When I looked at the end of the bed, I saw a blacker than black shadow. It was six feet tall in and the shape of a man. I know that because the ceiling was about seven and a half foot tall. This room was about 22 by 25 feet. Again, the bed was up against the wall and at the end of bed was this blacker than black shadow. The only light in the room was this small TV.

I thought, "Oh my God, someone's in the room." Then, I realized a person in the room made no sense. Why didn't he have any mouth? Why couldn't I see clothes? Why couldn't I see skin? It was looking at me. It kind of tilted its head from side to side, and I just got more and more frightened. It was so hard for me to breathe because I couldn't open my mouth. It felt like there were two straws in my nose I was breathing through and I couldn't move. Now mind you, I'm not on my back and I'm not on my side, I'm kind of midway. I kept thinking, "Oh my God! What am I seeing? What am I seeing?" Then it disappeared. I was beyond scared, the most scared I've ever been in my entire life.

My eyes were going everywhere, trying to look for this thing. I kept asking myself, "Is it going to kill me? Why can't I scream? Why isn't my boyfriend waking up? Why can't he feel this?" Then, I looked up, and to my utter horror, I see this thing crouched in what I'd describe is a Spiderman crouch. You know, when he crouches with his hand between his knees, and his knees are kind of bowed out? It stuck to the ceiling and it was looking at me with its head is going side to side, and all I could think of was that it was feeding off my fear. I still couldn't breathe, I thought I was going to die. I couldn't move. I was looking up at this thing and screaming at the top of my lungs on the inside. This thing now came racing towards me with its hand outstretched, and I felt it plop on the bed in between me and my boyfriend.

I could feel this thing lying on me with its head on top of my ear. I could feel it cuddle up behind me. I don't recall if it was cold or hot, all I know is that I was absolutely screaming at the top of my lungs, again on the inside. I felt its head rest against my head, and I saw a hand come in front of my face and go over my mouth. For that few seconds that I saw the hand go over my mouth I noticed that its fingers were webbed like another super-hero, Aquaman!

I felt the pressure on the bed behind me and it was covering my mouth. There are no words on this planet to describe how absolutely petrified I was, and how I thought I was going to die. Finally, out of nowhere I thought of calling on God. I said, "Jesus please help me. Jesus help me. Help me. Help me Jesus." Poof, it was gone, and I could move. I sat up and screamed. I sat up out of breath and got my shoes. I said, "I've got to go. I've got to go, I can't." My boyfriend asked, "What's wrong? What's wrong?" I said, "Nothing, nothing, I've got to get out of here." I never went back to that place ever again. It was awful. Talking about it even now gives me the chills.

—Lilly, Massachusetts

35

They Hate the Church Music, Mommy

Earlier, I told you about the evil shadow figure who visited me. This experience happened about four or five years later and my boyfriend and I had married. At this time, my son was about three-years-old and we moved into this second floor apartment maybe twenty blocks away from that place. It was toward the center of town. We had a lot of problems there. We talk about it now just because we happen to watch ghost shows, but a lot of bad stuff happened in that house.

My husband was still working the graveyard shift. This night, I was in bed and I woke up and I felt the same terror I described in my earlier story. I opened my eyes and I thought, "Oh my God, not again." This time was different. This figure was taller than the window in the bedroom and I noticed it was much more muscular. It had kind of pointed ears, like "Spock ears." It paced back and forth in front of the bed. I couldn't move.

Then, not with my ears, but almost telepathically, I heard a mechanical type voice say, "You're not seeing what you're seeing. Go back to sleep. You're not seeing what you're seeing. Go back to sleep." It just kept repeating that. I was so petrified. Again, I couldn't breathe. I thought, "I'm going to die. This thing is going to kill me. I have a son in the mix now. I believe I'm dealing with this." I heard my son sobbing from his room, "Mommy, Mommy, there's something in my room." I took the initiative. I thought, "Oh hell no, not my child. Not my baby."

Somehow, I willed myself out of that paralyzed state. I flew out of bed, ran to my son's side, and I told him, "It's OK baby, it's OK." I prayed with him, and I commanded whatever it was, "You leave in the name of Jesus." I was a born-again Christian at that time. I said, "Whatever you are, you get out of here. You have no right over me or my son." My son said, "Mommy, put the church music on. They hate the church music." My heart dropped. I thought how long has he seen these things? So, I immediately ran and I put his little *Sleep Sound in Jesus* cassette tape on and the room felt lighter.

I never saw that thing again, but we had a lot of bad experiences in that house. We lost keys, had nightmares, and so on. Fast forward to about five years ago, and we're in the house that I'm in now. Again, I was in bed and I was lying on my side this time. I was facing my huge bedroom mirror that I have on the dresser and I got that feeling. I thought, "Oh God, not again, not again." I opened my eyes and I couldn't move. I looked in the mirror and saw standing in the doorway a woman-shaped figure. The only way I could describe the shape was to liken it to the silhouette from *Charlie's Angels* introduction? I saw that it was a woman because of the shape of the body, but her hair was like Medusa with a bunch of wavy hair snake type things. Again, it was extremely dark. Then, I saw a grin and I knew there were teeth in there. It was horrible. It stood in the doorway and it felt like it was feeding off of my fear, as the others did. I knew what to do. I started to pray and tell it to leave in the name of Jesus. It left and I could move again.

Some of the experiences I've had, I'd never wish on anyone. I wanted to share my story because I want people to know. I'm not a bible thumper trying to push my religion on anyone, but if you're going through these things, you can call on your faith and ask for help. In my experience, you can usually get rid of the problem that way.

—*Lilly, Massachusetts*

36

A Meeting with Death

Note from Jim: While this storyteller was sharing her story on the Campfire podcast, we got disconnected and had to reconnect her call . . . it could have just been a bad connection. Or, maybe it was something else?

I was about nineteen-years-old, and two of my friends and I had rented our first place. One evening, we had a few friends over and one of them brought a Ouija board. This wasn't your typical department store Ouija board, this one was antique-looking. It had its original box, and it had the name William Fuld on it.

I later learned, about a decade later, the story of William Fuld, who was the father of the modern Ouija board and that made this whole thing even freakier. We knew it was an antique board, as it was definitely old. Judging from what I've seen on the Internet, it looked like this board was probably the 1930s edition.

Anyhow, we got the Ouija board out. My friend and I decided to be the ones to move the planchette around. None of our friends would believe it wasn't one of us pushing the planchette as we were receiving answers. So I said, "One of us will just get on it alone, and then I'll ask it a question that I don't know the answer to, like your mother's maiden name." Well, it wouldn't work with just one person. So, our solution was that my friend and I got back on the board together, and then we asked it a question that only one other person in the room knew. It was the maiden name of our friend's grandmother, something like that. We both closed our eyes, proving that we couldn't even see where the letters were on the board. Unbeknownst to me, my friend took her hand off of the planchette after I closed my eyes. When I opened them, I looked across the table and my friend's hands were up in the air. Everybody's jaw was on the floor. Apparently, I spelled the name entirely by myself, correctly, with my eyes closed. So, now we all pretty much realized it was working, that we're talking to something.

We asked it, "Who are you? What's your name?" It spelled the name Death. I said, "Your name is Death?" It said, "Yes." We said OK and asked him a couple questions. Then "Death" spells out, "Meet me on 100th and Aurora." That was an intersection that was only four blocks from where we were. We were on 97th and just a block down from Aurora Avenue. It was about midnight, we're nineteen-year-olds, and no one wanted to go. Everyone said, "What are you talking about? You're talking about going to meet Death."

I bluffed my friends and I said, "Well, if you guys aren't going to do it, I'm going to do it myself, and I might not come back and you'll feel terrible." So they all agreed to go and I said, "I'll buy us sodas. I'll buy us candies when we get up to the grocery store."

There was a grocery store at that particular intersection. So, we headed out and we're walking down Aurora towards 100th. Of course, we're waiting for the ground to swallow us whole, for a telephone pole to fall on us, or a Metro to go out of control and take us all out. Nothing happened, and we made it to the grocery store. We got the candy and the soda. Then, we had to make the trek back and come back past 100th and Aurora. Now, we were even anticipating it more, because this was his last chance, since he said he was going to meet us on 100th and Aurora.

We made it all the way back home and nothing happened. It didn't even start raining, and we're in Seattle, so that's a rare event. Maybe he did that for us, I don't know. We got back on the board and "Death" came through, and I said, "Are you there?" It said, "Yes." I said, "We went to 100th and Aurora, where were you?" It started to spell, "H-A-H-A-H-A." At first we couldn't figure it out, it took us about thirty seconds and then I looked up and said, "He's laughing. He's laughing!" We were so absolutely petrified that we didn't use the board ever again. Our impression was that he was really tickled that he was able to actually get us to do something. He told us to do something, and we did it.

I do believe that we were speaking with an entity. There are probably other occasions where the planchette is moved telekinetically and probably subconsciously, but I don't think that was the case, this time.

The question that was answered where the name was spelled correctly, that was particularly strange. I didn't know that name. As I mentioned, my eyes were closed and I was moving the planchette on the board by myself, which I didn't even realize at the time. It turns out that my friend on the board took her fingers off as soon as I closed my eyes. Believe me Jim, I would much rather believe that it was telekinetic, because I was left on the board alone and we all know what happened to little Regan in *The Exorcist.*

Retelling this story and the fact we were hung up on has given me the chills. I'm so freaking out right now, and I'm glad my husband's coming home soon!

—*Tracy, Washington*

37

It Lives Behind that Door

This story revolves around a friend of mine and it started before I ever visited her home. She had an experience with a presence while we were talking on the phone. It was so real that I thought someone had broken into her home. The way she was responding to whatever it was, made me think that somebody else was in her house and that she was being murdered. There was screaming and heavy breathing. I was ready to call 911, and she told me not to because it wasn't human.

We had a conversation about that and so I was apprised of the situation. By the time I went to visit her, I had steeled myself to the fact that there was something in her house. At the same time, I'm a sane person and what do you believe? I held out the possibility that it was her imagination or maybe she was under a lot of stress.

During this initial visit, I definitely felt something the first evening. Over the next few months of visiting, I experienced a lot more. My first direct experience with this presence was in her basement. The basement was very large, and there were several rooms down there including a home theater. She actually pointed out the room where she felt the presence stayed. The door was always closed to that room, and it was where she kept all of her Christmas and Halloween decorations.

The room looked creepy. Her dog and I were down in the home theater this particular evening, waiting for her to come downstairs. We were going to watch a movie on her projector. The dog started growling and looking at the door. This was just a little min pin. I got up and started distracting the dog. I was playing ball with her. We were in another part of the basement when my friend came down. We were getting ready to watch this movie and she pointed to the door to the decoration storage room. It was open. The door had been closed when she went upstairs. She told me the door would just randomly open, and she always knew that the presence in her home was more prominent when this door was open.

I was still in disbelief, taking it with a grain of salt, but at the same time the dog was growling and I didn't know what to make of that. It was strange. Dogs and animals, in general, can sense this kind of activity a lot easier than we can. Another strange thing about that weird room was that I couldn't get her dog to stay in it. Her dog would come in, get wild-eyed, and run back out.

Then, more stuff started to happen. She lives in Tennessee and I live in Oregon. I had made several trips back and forth. Once, she called me at home and told me that pictures of me had mysteriously flown off her mantle. They ended up in the middle of the room on the floor. Obviously, she didn't do that. You have things moving, you have animals being frightened, and you have the person who lives in the house saying that the thing lives there. It was quite a confluence of events.

One night, I was walking through her house on my way from one room to another. To the left of me, was the kitchen doorway, and as I walked past it, I saw a shadow figure. I turned around and stood there for a second, and it didn't move. It was just standing there looking at me with no shame. It was very, very creepy. I had never seen anything like that before. It was very tall, very wide, and very present. I think it was telling me, in essence, "This is my kitchen."

I can't remember which visit it was, but stuff continued to happen. I was asleep one night and I woke up to the blankets being pulled off of me. There was nobody there, but they were just coming off of me as if some invisible force was at work.

My friend was OK with whatever it was. She said that when I or when other people weren't around, it didn't really have a negative effect on her. She said that things seemed to ramp up when other people were around. It didn't welcome visitors and my friend had the idea that "it" wanted her all to itself. It was very, very creepy.

The last time I visited was two years ago. On the last couple of visits nothing happened. After my pictures flew off of the mantel, I told her the next time I visited I would bring sage with me. My plan was to burn the sage in her house and see if that would help things die down or help to get rid of it.

On that next visit, I came into the house and handed her some sage. I said that we were going to burn it and tell this presence that it needed to go because it wasn't welcome anymore. I told her, "You really need to be on board with this, too." So, we walked around her very large house, went into that little room, and burned a lot of sage. Then, we went to go to sleep. We were in her room and when we were ready to fall asleep, we heard two different doors open in the basement. We were in her very dark house still hearing activity going on.

This entity felt separate. It wasn't like anything my friend would have been generating. I've been in situations where I've seen poltergeist activity, and it tends to be prevalent in adolescents because of their energy. When I was an adolescent, there was a lot of poltergeist activity around me and my sister, who was also going through puberty around the same time. This felt different from that, because there was more than just the stuff moving. I was walking through my friend's bedroom one time on my way back to her living area. Something whispered right in my ear, "Get out." That's not poltergeist activity, neither was the shadow figure or the dog being freaked out, they're all a little different. This was a very ominous, weird, and malevolent-feeling presence.

—*Lisa, Oregon*

38

Weird, Wonderful West Virginia

This experience was probably the most formative one in my emotional development as a child. It happened when I was eight-years-old. Two of my older siblings and I witnessed something inexplicable. We had recently moved from Lorain, Ohio to southern West Virginia, the heart of rural Appalachia.

We were what you'd call "urban Appalachians." My parents originally were from Southern West Virginia, the Mingo County area which is known popularly as the stomping ground of the famous feuding families of the Hatfields and McCoy. As children we had never visited, but we moved there after a family tragedy in 1971. My eldest sister was killed in an automobile accident and my parents wanted to be closer to their immediate family. The family offered emotional support and my parents needed it. I was the youngest of the siblings.

The rural poverty there was truly incomprehensible to me and my siblings. We'd never seen anything of that magnitude and it was just an unbelievable experience. We moved into a home that was about half a mile down the creek from our Uncle Walker, my father's eldest brother, who found the house for us. We were coming from an urban northern Ohio community. Lorain was working class, but still within mainstream American society, as opposed to an area where we really thought, and I hate to say this, people were very backward culturally. Unfortunately, we brought a lot of that prejudice with us.

When we started going to school, each of us were asked by our classmates if we had seen any ghosts in our new house. We thought that these people were not really with it. We didn't believe them and we thought that they were culturally backwards. We told them that no that we hadn't seen any ghosts and we asked them to please knock it off, but they were persistent. They'd ask, "Have you seen any ghosts in your house?" We could truthfully say no until this one day I'll always remember.

This area was very rural. We had the only home within a one-mile radius, and we were in this very remote area on a hillside. Our uncle was our nearest neighbor, as I said, about a half mile up the creek from us.

On this Sunday, my parents had gone into town, Matewan, with one of my sisters to shop for groceries. It was an afternoon that I remember very well. I was eight, my brother was ten, the older sisters who'd stayed behind were thirteen and fourteen. We were all sitting in the living room watching television and playing a board game on the floor.

We had a dog, Mitten, chained up to the front porch, on an eight to ten foot chain. We had our front door open. All of a sudden, Mitten began barking hysterically. This was a very protective dog and he began barking and growling to an extent that we had never heard. My brother and I jumped up to the front door. We were like our family's little men, as my mom used to call us, when my dad was gone. So, we ran up to the front door to look out the door thinking that either a human or a bear was about to come into the yard.

To this day, I still give myself a shiver when I think about it. My brother and I quickly looked out the door towards the direction that our dog Mitten was barking. Outside standing at the corner of the house was this figure, and we could only see his front half. His back half was around the corner of the house. He was standing as straight as a soldier and it was obvious that it was a human figure. We thought that it was a person standing there, knowing that our father was not home, attempting to play some sort of game with us in some way.

We yelled at him and by then, my eldest sister had run to the front door. We were at the front door yelling at him to not come into the house because we had a gun and we would defend ourselves. My sister said, "And I'll use it." I remember that very clearly. He was still standing there when my sister ran back to my parent's bedroom and retrieved one of my father's handguns.

My father told us to never get into his guns, and we took him at his word. We never played with his guns. It was a very serious subject around our house. Anyway, my sister came back from the bedroom with the gun in her hand. When she got to the door, this thing moved away from the house. It moved down our gravel driveway, and its shape was reminiscent of what you would describe as a rain slicker with a full body rain cap. The figure was something you would see like a silhouette of a New England style fisherman type outfit. It was completely flat black, there was no light reflection off of it whatsoever. This was not a shadow or an optical illusion. All three of us saw it.

As it moved away from the house, it was floating above the ground and down the gravel driveway. Our dog was following it with his eyes as well, barking at it. As it was floating, there were no feet that were obvious, and it was not making any sound whatsoever. When it reached the end of the driveway, it made a right-hand turn at the bushes where they met the road.

We were in shock after this event, and when my parents and other sister got home, we told them what happened. Our mother believed us, but our dad did not. He was very pragmatic and very much in the here-and-now type thing. His opinion was that we just saw something that was explicable.

About two weeks later, the story continued. After we had all gone to school, my mom liked to sit on the front porch in the mornings after a nice rain. This day we had all left and she was sitting on the front porch when she saw the same figure. Mom said it came up out of the ground, where the roadway met the driveway. Instead of going down the driveway like we had seen, it came up the driveway toward the house. When we saw it floating there, it was like looking at a stick figure almost moving down the driveway. There was no body motion. My mother said that when she saw it come up the driveway, it was very animated. Running, as if kicking its legs up very high, moving the garment that it had over it. She thought it was going to come up the steps, but it proceeded up past the corner of the house. She said that it was also floating above the ground about a foot. It was not touching the ground. When she told us this, we thought, "Yes, we know now."

These kids at school who we thought were so culturally backward? They weren't as backward as we thought they were, because they were obviously on to something that we had not known about when we moved there.

About two weeks after my mother's experience, most of us had gone to bed at night at about eleven. My mother and my sister, the one who had originally gone to Matewan with my parents when the figure first appeared, were cleaning up the kitchen. They were the only ones up. All of a sudden, there came incredible noise from our attic. It literally sounded as though all heck was breaking loose up there. It was incredible. It sounded as though somebody started stomping through glass and turning over furniture. There was almost nothing in this unfinished attic. It had no furniture except an ironing board with an iron sitting on it. Still, there were the most incredible noises coming from our attic. That woke us all, if we were not already awake. My mom ran into the bedroom to get my dad. He was awake and already had a handgun with him. My oldest brother, who was eighteen at the time, came out of his room. He and my dad armed themselves. I still admire my dad to this day for the courage he demonstrated. He and my oldest brother stood at the bottom of the stairs, and my dad yelled upstairs. He thought somebody had broken in, as we all did.

We were not thinking anything otherworldly about this, even though we'd had these experiences. My father yelled, "Whoever's up there, I'm giving you one chance to get out. I'm armed and I'm coming up the steps. I'm giving you one chance to get out." It still sounded as if somebody was running through glass. Well, he was going to fire his handgun up the stairs. He did not want to confront and possibly shoot somebody. He attempted to fire his handgun up these steps, and it misfired two or three times. My dad knew how to care for his guns and he occasionally test-fired in a rural area, so these were working weapons.

My dad still went up the steps. As he got to the top of the

stairs, he opened the door. As soon as he did, it was like a bad horror movie. He opened that door and everything stopped. All the noises stopped completely. He expected to see the worst commotion in the attic. Mind you, when we all went up there afterward, even the cobwebs were still in the windowsill. There was no disturbance whatsoever. We stayed at the house not much longer than another week or two. It was always planned to be temporary and then we relocated to another area.

I say this now as an almost fifty-year-old person, that that was a very formative part of my development as a child. I stuttered, partly I think, because of this incident, until I was 13 years old. I taught myself not to stutter by controlling my breathing, but I know these events traumatized me as a child. To this day, it's still a very impactful part of my history and it all happened in Southern West Virginia.

—*David, Oregon*

39

Fuzzy Wuzzy Was a . . . Demon

This goes back to the mid-seventies when I was in college. I had a pretty close friend who I'll call Paul. He was a gregarious guy and liked to party a lot. He seemed to have a lot of friends around him and was one of these guys who seemed to have a lot of girlfriends. It seemed like every month he would change girlfriends, I don't think he was shallow or anything. We were in college and he just hadn't settled down yet.

He got involved with a girl, whom I had never met. I remember him saying that she was getting a little too clingy and he didn't like that. He was considering breaking up with her. One night, she invited him over to her apartment and she introduced him to several of her friends who she said were in a coven of witches that she was involved in herself. They brought out a Ouija board and had a séance with this demon that they supposedly worshipped.

They gave the demon a kind of cutesy name. I'm not going to repeat it verbatim because I'm still just marginally freaked out about it. Let's just say the name was similar to Fuzzy Wuzzy.

Anyway, the essence of the séance was that Paul couldn't leave this girl or he would make the demon angry. Now, he was a skeptic like me so he laughed the whole thing off. They told him that he couldn't tell a soul about it because it was their secret. He just thought they were messing with his head so he told me and all of his friends. He said, "Man, I was hanging out with these weird girls. They thought they were witches and they thought they worshipped this demon named Fuzzy Wuzzy."

Eventually, it turned out that it wasn't very funny. Paul worked in a convenience store on the night shift and he was mostly there by himself. After some time, he started telling people that strange things were happening while he was there by himself. He'd hear his name being called behind him, he'd turn, and no one would be there. He'd feel a tap on his shoulder, turn, and no one was there. We kind of humored him thinking that these girls had just messed with his head.

He found out that they had put a curse on him because he told everybody the name of this demon and laughed at them. Eventually, the incidents started getting weirder and Paul started looking bad, like he was losing sleep. He wasn't taking care of himself. He said he would hear things like wings flapping at him in the store and nothing would be there. Then one night, he was sweeping up and the broom handle broke in his hands for no particular reason. I think the creepiest thing he mentioned that occurred was one night when he was walking home from the store. A dog followed him from a distance of twenty or thirty feet, which is a little weird for a dog. Usually, a dog will either come up and say hello and try to make friends, or they'll growl and bark. Generally, they don't stalk you.

None of his friends ever saw any of this though, it was just stuff he was telling us. It was completely atypical of him. I saw some of this play out one weekend when both he and I were staying on campus and it was totally deserted. He didn't want to stay by himself, so I invited him over to my dorm. We sat and talked a while. He had quit his job at the convenience store. He just couldn't stand being there by himself. As we were discussing his options, a book sort of arced off my bookshelf and landed in the floor. That actually didn't frighten me that much, believe it or not. However, Paul's reaction did. He laughed almost hysterically, "Ha, ha, ha, aha, ha, you saw that, didn't you? You saw that. Did you see it?" I assured him that yes, I did see it. For some reason, I had to keep it together because he was borderline hysterical about this. It would enhance the story if I could tell you that the book fell off the shelf and landed on some significant page, but it didn't really. It was my old chemistry book from high school, and I think it landed on a page about the chemical element Boron or something. I couldn't deduce any significance from that.

I looked at the shelf thoroughly and there was nothing, like a string or anything, where our friends would have been playing tricks on us. The book was too heavy for a mouse or something to have kicked it. It would have taken a rat and we surely would have noticed something that large.

The weird thing is that I think after that night when someone else finally saw what was happening to him, we discussed it and I told Paul, "OK, I think a lot of this may be coming from you. I mean, the curse is on you, somehow it's coming from your mind. And even if it is a demon, it's not a very powerful demon if all it can do is knock a book off a shelf."

Maybe what happened here was, not that they successfully put a spell on him, but that they so convinced him that they had, that he was creating this phenomenon. There was something about it mainly happening when he was alone. To the credit of all his friends, we humored him because we could tell that he was distressed. I think the very act of someone else seeing it and reassuring him that it wasn't going to hurt him, helped Paul. Right afterward, he got some badly needed sleep and from what I understand, nothing ever happened again. Still, to this day, I don't understand how that book arced off the shelf and landed on the floor. I was there and saw it, but I have no explanation for that.

—*Kevin, Tennessee*

Jim Harold

40

A Shocking Shadow

This happened back when I was attending school in Chicago. The school had just bought an old hotel building right down in The Loop, and converted it into dormitories. At the time, I had a boyfriend and he also lived in a dorm. He had a fairly boisterous roommate who had a lot of visitors, so when my roommate was away, my boyfriend would stay over.

We had bunk beds in the dorms with desks underneath. This night, we smushed into the bunk bed, which was obviously really small and he fell asleep right away. I was a bit of an insomniac and it would take me awhile to fall asleep, so I ended up just lying there and thinking. I noticed something strange. I was looking up at the ceiling, and all of a sudden in the corner of it, right above my head, this black shadow appeared. I thought, "Oh, it must be someone maybe out in the hall, and the shadow's falling under the door and somehow managing to get into the room." So I peeked over the bed and there was no one there. Nothing was flashing by the door. I looked back up and the shadow was getting larger. I thought that was pretty odd.

The single window faced the brick wall of another building and we always had the blinds down anyway, so there wasn't any light coming through there. The more I looked at the shadow, the more it started to seem really strange. It started moving across the ceiling, getting darker and darker, blacker and blacker. It began to almost look like as if someone spilled a bottle of ink. It was such a deep black that you couldn't mistake what it was. It started spreading across the ceiling, and that's when I began to put two and two together. It wasn't not normal. As it got bigger, I got scared.

The shadow was almost over the whole bed and I nudged my boyfriend to wake up. I'd never had paranormal experiences at the time. The most I'd ever heard of were apparitions, ghosts and maybe poltergeists. I'd never heard of things like shadow people or anything else of the sort. I didn't know what I was witnessing. As soon as I started to nudge my boyfriend to wake up, the figure shot back into itself and disappeared right back into the corner of the ceiling where it had come from. I had been watching it the whole time. My boyfriend finally woke and I told him what I saw. He started doing the old, "Oh, you were just dreaming" routine. I said, "No, no, no. I hadn't even fallen asleep, and I'm checking the door and looking down and making sure there's no shadows." He said, "Go back to sleep. Go back to sleep."

Well, I was definitely scared. He fell right back to sleep, and I was lying there very still. I put the covers over my head and it felt like a five-year-old who thinks, "If I lie really, really still, it won't know I'm here. It won't come back." I don't know how long I was like that, but eventually I ended up falling asleep.

Here is where it gets even weirder. I had a dream and it was very lucid, very vivid. In it, I was standing in the same dorm room.

Everything was exactly as it was in real life, except the lights were on and I was standing by the door. My boyfriend was up in the bunk bed and he was yelling at me, but I couldn't hear what he was saying. Everything was happening in slow motion.

Eventually, sound started coming through and I could hear him saying. "Turn off the light. Turn off the light." I looked at him and said, "What do you mean?" He said, "Turn off the light before it gets you." In my dream, I turned toward the light switch that was by the door, and that black inky thing was moving across the wall. As I reached for the light to turn it off, the black inky thing reached the light switch at the same time, and as I touched the light switch, it touched me. As soon as it touched me, I felt this massive shock of electricity go through me. I started falling backwards in slow motion in my dream. As I fell backward, I woke up.

There I was, lying in the bed, in pitch darkness, unable to move. I was completely frozen. That shock was still going up and down my body, back and forth, back and forth. I tried to scream and I tried to move my hands. I couldn't. I have no idea how long that feeling lasted. It felt like it was five minutes, but it could have been one. By the time I got my voice back, I started yelling. At the very same time, my boyfriend started yelling and he shot up in bed.

I was trying to tell him what just happened and he was trying to tell me something too. Finally, he told me that he had been dreaming a vivid dream, too. In it, the black thing that I had told him about was moving across the covers of the bed. In his dream, it had gotten under the covers and touched him. When that happened, he said he got shocked by what he described as electricity. It the same type of feeling I had! When that happened, he woke up but he couldn't move or speak either.

He said he felt that same pulse of electricity going back-and-forth on his body, and as soon as he had feeling come back, he started yelling. That was the same time I got the feeling back in my body and I started yelling. We grabbed my pillows and my covers then spent the rest of the weekend in his dorm room with his crazy roommate. I had a few days where I was afraid to be in the dorm room by myself, but eventually that feeling passed. I never had that experience again in the dorm room.

Years later, I ran into someone who had been living in the building that same year on a different floor. I believe we were at a Halloween party and we were swapping weird stories. She said, "Oh my God, I've had experiences in that building too." She was in a single room and would sleep the whole year with her door wide open because she would see things in her room out of the corner of her eye. It was kind of good, if spooky, to hear that someone else had weird experiences there.

It seemed there were some spirits lurking about in that old hotel. I heard that someone had seen an apparition of a girl in the lounge on the top floor that same year. This was before my experience when I was a skeptic and I kind of brushed it off at the time. I'm sure there were definitely strange things that happened. The building must have been over 100-years-old because it was right downtown and there are a lot of old buildings nearby.

I think this entity would have done physical harm to me if it had the chance. I absolutely do. In a way, I feel that we were attacked physically, but I think it could have been worse. It was spooky. I would have passed it off as night paralysis had it not happened to my boyfriend at the same time.

—*Julita, Connecticut*

41
Skinwalker

round 1993, I was working security at a hotel here in Taos, New Mexico on the graveyard shift. It was a beautiful, summer night and I was relaxing in my car. It was a 1978 Thunderbird, one of those big, heavy cars from the old days. I started to get a little bit sleepy, and suddenly something punched the bottom of the car. I mean it was a LOUD thump. It startled me, my eyes popped open, and I reached for my pistol on the seat. It rattled me that much. I started the car, pulled forward, whipped around in the parking lot, and to my surprise there was a dog-looking thing sitting where my car was parked. It was staring at me, and what freaked me out the most about it, was its eyes. It had these almost human characteristics in its gaze, and I could almost feel like my soul was being invaded. This was not a regular dog.

Still, it was on all fours and ran like a regular dog. It freaked me out so badly I really didn't know what to do, so I hit it the gas pedal to see if I could either hit it with the car or scare it off. It ran across the highway onto Taos Pueblo property, and then I saw it whip back across toward the units that were there. The hotel I worked at was kind of a sprawling place and I chased it in the car and it went into parking lot number three. There's a place there called The Ponds. It has cesspool areas and the weeds there grow to be about ten feet tall. I put my headlights on bright and I kept the car running.

I got out and pursued this thing in the weeds. I came up to the top of a hill in this weedy area, and I couldn't see diddly squat, but I could hear this thing moving around. It sounded like it was trying to come out behind me. I tried to maneuver around behind it and to stay close to the top of the hill. Just then, something pushed behind me, knocked me to the ground, and threw me like I was nothing. I stood up and scrambled for my pistol. I had to search around for it and then I grabbed it. I stood up and I saw something running on two legs. It looked like a nude man, and it ran across a patch of sagebrush toward some houses. I wanted to take a shot at it to see what it would do, not to kill it, but I couldn't because I thought it might be a guy, a human being. I heard a scream coming from the direction the thing ran. It didn't sound human, but it didn't sound animal either. It sounded like a combination of the two which was bizarre. It was the type of scream that would almost cause loss of bowel control and it scared me pretty badly.

I've never seen anything like that before or since.

I've had some weird occurrences and witnessed some strange things in that hotel. Some of the guests had complained about something walking around, jiggling their doorknobs. I'd either be in my car patrolling the area or on foot, but I never saw anybody doing anything. Still, I'd always get reports the next morning. I had told some of my coworkers what had happened to me that night, and they were not the least bit surprised. A lot of them were Native Americans from Taos Pueblo that I had either grown up with my whole life or knew very well, and they weren't at all surprised. They said, "Oh, you saw a skinwalker." I said, "A skinwhat?" They told me what it was. They said, "You saw a skinwalker. It's an evil being that's able to move between the world we know and the dark world. He's able to shape shift. He can either appear as a coyote, a wolf, or a dog. If you allow him to, he'll suck the soul right out of you. And, to see one is usually bad luck." Needless to say, I thought about it long and hard. I looked around a lot of corners after that.

I didn't have a bad run of luck or anything after this experience. I think that the reason that it didn't have a lot of power over me is that I didn't show any fear. I felt fear, but I was some type of knucklehead at the time to go chasing it into the weeds like that. I had just gotten out of the service, so I was a pretty gutsy guy. I had a pistol with me so I thought . . . well, I don't really know what I was thinking. I should have just left well enough alone. What surprised me also was the way it hit and rocked my car. That was very heavy to move and yet it felt like it exerted very little effort to do it. Like I said, it was a '78 T-bird.

I'm not as young as I used to be and with age comes wisdom. I doubt that I would pursue anything like that ever again.

—*John, New Mexico*

42
Evil Me

During my senior year of high school, my parents added a bathroom to our unfinished basement. After the work began, weird stuff started happening. At first, they were just little things. For example, my dad had three tape measures and all three disappeared. We'd find them in weird places, like behind the dog food and in the yard.

I'd see shadows, but I would always just tell myself that it was just my imagination. This went on the entire time they were working on the project. It came to a head this one evening when I woke up in the middle of the night and had to go to the bathroom. The downstairs bathroom wasn't finished yet so I went upstairs. Out of habit, I glanced into the bathroom mirror and I saw myself but I looked different. The best way I can describe it is that I saw an evil version of myself. I don't know. It was so creepy. My eyes weren't right. They were too dark and too hard. You know when you look at someone and they're not smiling, but their eyes are?

That's kind of what I looked like in this mirror, but it wasn't a nice smile. It was just really scary. So, I left the bathroom and I went into the kitchen. I thought maybe I was just tired or that I had sleep in my eyes. I took a drink of water, washed my face, and took a deep breath. I went back into the bathroom and again it was "Evil Bailey" staring back at me in the mirror. "She" was still there.

I was really freaked out at this point and I don't think I've ever been that scared in my entire life. The mirror in this bathroom has three panes, and one of them is flat against the wall. There's one on either side, set at angles. The center pane was the one I had been looking into. I looked in the left pane and it was still "Evil Bailey," and then I looked in the right pane and it was normal me. I just looked tired and scared, but it was normal me. In the left and in the center one it was still "Evil Bailey." After that, I just went back downstairs and back to bed.

"Evil Bailey" was me, but her eyes were too dark. I have green eyes, but in the mirror they looked almost like brown or black. They were too narrow and too long. I have a somewhat round face, but her features were sharper with sharper cheekbones and jawline. It was me, just freaky and different. I don't really know what it was.

About a week later, my dad finished the bathroom downstairs and nothing happened for two or three years. Everything was quiet until I came back during my sophomore year of college for Christmas break. I came home to find my parents were completely renovating the house. Walls were torn down and new drywall was being put up. Everything was being redone with new carpet, new hardwood floors, and windows being put where there weren't any before. The house looked completely different. Since they were still working on the renovations, it was a construction site.

I was usually the only one home during the day, since my parents both worked and my brothers were both still in high school. I'd be sitting in the living room with my pets and they would start acting weird. The cats would jump up, screech and run out of the room. My dog, who does not have a mean bone in her body, would suddenly sit up and start to growl. The hair was standing up on her back. It was really strange since I was the only one in the house.

I really trust my animals to know what's going on, even if we don't. So, their reactions were worrisome. I would see weird shadows just out of the corner of my eye, but I could never quite catch what they were. I tried really hard to explain them away. I rationalized that maybe since the house had changed so much that I wasn't used to where the shadows fell.

When I'd hear weird knocks or noises somewhere in the house, I'd assume that the airflow in the house was different from what I was used to and that might explain it. I tried really hard to come up with good rationales for what was going on, but sometimes I just couldn't.

One day, I was walking downstairs into the basement and I heard a conversation between two voices. One sounded kind of female, and the other kind of male. This was just for a few seconds and they didn't really sound very happy. In fact, they sounded like they were arguing. I could feel the breath of their voices in my right ear. When I stopped to listen, they stopped too. It was as though I walked in on their conversation and they stopped arguing. I listened for a couple more minutes and didn't hear anything, so I went back upstairs. I had no idea what it was. I thought I might be having some type of ear spasm.

A couple days later my dad was away on work, so it was just me, my mom and my brothers in the house. I woke up in the middle of the night because I had a dream that someone was in our house who wasn't supposed to be. It felt so real that I got up and I found my brother's baseball bat. I checked the house, but nothing was out of the ordinary so I just went back to bed. Then I had the dream again, and I got up and I checked the house one more time. Nothing was out of place. So I went back to bed. Finally, I had the dream a third time, but the this time I didn't get up. I just rolled over and went back to sleep because I figured that I was just freaking myself out. I woke up in the morning and I told my mom about my dream. She kind of got a little freaked out. I asked, "What's wrong?" She said, "Well, your brother had that same dream last night." She thought that someone actually had been in our house. We checked everything, all the windows, the doors, but everything was absolutely normal. That freaked my mom out a little bit.

Then things came to a head a couple of days later. My dad was supposed to be coming home later that night. It was about 11 a.m. in the morning and I was in the kitchen alone in the house washing dishes. To my right, I heard two footsteps. I stopped to look and nothing was there, so I went back to washing dishes. Almost immediately, I heard two more footsteps and they were closer. Again, I stopped and nothing was there. So I started back up while looking out of the corner of my eye and I heard two more. These were so close to me that I could feel the vibrations on the floor through my feet. I was so startled that I dropped the plate that I was washing, and I ran into the living room. I should say you can see the kitchen from there. I waited a couple of minutes. Then, all of a sudden, I saw this shadow on the wall in front of me go from the left to the right. About two seconds later, I heard this growl behind me go in the opposite direction from the right to the left. I thought there was someone there. I said, "Hello, who's there?" I didn't hear anything. A couple minutes went by and I calmed down enough to go back into the kitchen and continue washing dishes. When I got there, I saw that the plate I had dropped on the floor was sitting on the edge of the counter! After that, I went back to the living room and sat in the corner where I could see everything until my mom got home. I was freaked out. I couldn't really explain away a plate that somehow picked itself up and put itself back on the counter!

Usually when I told my parents about something strange happening, they would give a logical explanation saying there are no such things as the paranormal. This time, I told my mom what was happening and instead of saying what she normally said, she remarked, "Honey, don't worry, we know everyone who has always lived in this house, and nothing bad ever happened to them." That was the last thing she said about it. Then I told my dad and he said almost the exact same thing. He said, "Don't worry, nothing bad has ever happened in this house." Instead of acting like I was silly, they both sort of acknowledged that it could be happening, and that struck me. After that, if anything happened, I completely ignored it. There's still been a couple of weird shadows or something. It always seems to wake up a little bit whenever we start to do renovations because not too long after the thing with the plate happened, our house was done, so it hasn't happened since. Maybe something or someone doesn't like it when we start tinkering with the house!

—Bailey, Wyoming

43

The Man in Red

He started to visit me when I was about nine years old. I lived in an apartment complex with my mom, my brothers, and my sisters. It was a very odd thing. A man in red would always come around three or four in the morning. I'd hear the door open. Our doors were always locked at night. My mom would never leave any open. I could see the hallway light, because it was an apartment building. I'd see the door open, and then all of a sudden, I'd see the light come into the apartment and I'd hear these very heavy, thumping footsteps coming into the living room. This strange man would sit on the small couch that my mom had in the living room. He'd just sit there for maybe half an hour. I was scared to death, as I was only nine years old. Right when he was about to turn his head and look towards my bedroom, I would just close my eyes, count to ten, start praying, and after a little while, he'd be gone. That was what happened all the way until I turned thirteen.

I'm convinced that this wasn't just a person. I think it was an entity of some type. He was really tall, he was about seven feet, and very creepy. It would always happen just around three or four. After a while, I started to tell my mom about it, but she would always say it was in my head. Then, my younger sister started having nightmares, and she said she would see this same figure coming in around three in the morning. It kind of sounded a little too familiar for me, so I started asking her a lot of questions. We'd stay up really late at night and try to see if he'd come and he would. Eventually not only did my younger sister see it, but friends that would sleep over saw him too. Then, they would never want to sleep over at my house again.

He'd just wander around and just sit on the couch. Once he would turn his head toward the bedroom, we'd all just scream and tuck underneath the blankets. This man wasn't like the classic picture of the devil with the red face and all of that, but he wasn't what I'd call normal either. He was really tall, really lanky. When he tried to come into a room, he'd have to bend over. That's how tall he was. You could tell it wasn't a normal person. He had a cloak, like an old monk's cloak, but it was huge, like a really deep red, almost a burgundy color. He kind of floated, so he didn't walk right.

My brothers, my sisters and I experienced a lot of activity in the house growing up, so we tried an experiment. We'd use a tape recorder and try to record things. We found some weird stuff on the tape, and we even contacted a priest over in Vatican City who wrote to us and was very nice. He sent the Archbishop to our house, and he blessed our home. Still, we always had strange activity in the house.

If my mom ever tried to light a candle, it would explode. Also, things would come up missing. One time my brother was with a friend in the house and the room all of a sudden got cloudy with a really thick fog. We had no idea what it was. His friend just freaked out, ran out the door, and he never came back. All kinds of stuff happened in the house.

I haven't seen this figure in a very long time, thank goodness, but we do have activity every now and then. It's not as severe as when we were younger. I wonder if anyone else out there has seen the man in red.

—Joselyn, Florida

44

The Little Nasties

My youngest brother Jack lived about two hours away from me when I lived in San Diego, and I used to regularly go to visit. After a third baby came along, I would sleep in the baby's room. Now, the adult bed in the room had belonged to the kids' deceased grandfather. During this particular visit, I had taken off work kind of early and driven up. I was tired so I just thought I'd just get a little catnap and I went in to lie down.

I don't know if your readers know about astral projection, but I think that might come into play here. There's this period that you go through when you go to sleep called the hypnagogic state and that is where you're kind of in between. Your mind is awake, but your body's asleep. When you're in that state, you kind of feel electrical pulses and stuff, and you can also see little entities sometimes. It can be very disconcerting.

I went to lie down to take this nap, and I was so tired I thought I would sleep well. I woke up but my body was asleep, and I could feel the electrical pulses and I got so frustrated. I was tired and couldn't get any rest. A lot of times when you're in that state, sometimes if you can wake yourself up at least enough to move, to turn over, it'll stop and you can go back to sleep or you'll just totally wake up. I tried doing that and it didn't work, so I just gave up on the nap.

Later that night, after staying up too late with my brother talking and carrying on, I was pretty exhausted and I crawled into—his name was Jerry—Jerry's old bed and I thought, "Well, I'm going to go right to sleep." Dang it, if I didn't wake up again in that state. This time was different though. Along with the electric pulses that were happening as I was half awake, I could see what I will call the little nasties, they're like these little creatures. I know it sounds crazy but I've seen them quite a few times. They're six inches high, and a lot of times they're red, and they have a little pitch fork. It almost looks like the Devil's Imps or something.

I don't know if it's because I project them to look like that, or if that's where humanity kind of got the look for the Devil. Anyway, they were jumping up and down on me and poking me and laughing. They were very annoying. I'd learned to not be afraid of them. I have a certain prayer that I say, and usually that dispels them, but they just weren't going away. So, this time I couldn't figure out what was going on. It was like they were purposely trying to keep me awake.

I finally got myself awake enough that I actually flipped and reoriented my body so my head was where my feet were before, so I could go back to sleep, but they still wouldn't leave me alone. After about two hours or so I finally passed out. I knew I had to go to sleep because my cereal sugar-filled nephews were going to be up in a few hours, and I was going to be in no shape for that!

I just couldn't understand why they were bothering me, because there had to be a reason. The next night I went to bed, and I was definitely going to pass out because I was so exhausted. However, the exact same thing happened. I could not figure it out. I changed all my positions again and finally I got up and said, "OK, it's got to be Jerry." I wondered if he was mad because I was sleeping in his bed? That would have been kind of stupid since we'd really never met. Then, I thought maybe he just thought I was just some strange woman in his grandson's bedroom and he was haunting me to get me out.

Eventually, I did fall asleep but during the whole drive home to San Diego, I was trying to figure out why this happened. I just couldn't come up with any good reason why this kept me up three times in a row, because that never happens to me. About a week or so went by, and my sister-in-law, Bernice, called and she wanted to give me the lowdown on what my nephews were doing to her. How the little terrors were torturing her in general, and it was funny. In the back of my head, I must have been thinking about the fact that I wasn't able to sleep at her house.

For some reason, I just blurted out to her, "Where is Jerry? I mean, his ashes." Because he had been cremated? My sister-in-law started laughing and sheepishly kind of said to me, "In our closet." I said, "That's it! He wants to be interred!" Oh my God, all of a sudden it made sense to me. I told her, I said, "Listen, he is pissed off and he wants to be with his wife." It was really weird, because I had never talked to Bernice about ghosts or other supernatural stuff that's happened to me, so I wasn't sure if she was going to laugh at me or think I'd gone around the bend. She actually believed it and I said, "He really wants to go." They took care of it within a week and I've never had any problems visiting there since. So, he was mad. He was really mad.

I just wish these spirits would be more clear about what they want or that there would be a consistent way it could be communicated. When you talk to psychics, it seems like they always know. They see them, hear them or something. For me, it's in a dream, or this one was in a hypnagogic state, and I wondered, "What the heck is that?" That was a first for me.

—*Sandy, California*

PART THREE

BEYOND EXPLANATION

45
Who's in that Coffin

This is the first dream I've ever had that was kind of a premonition, which I find fascinating.

In this dream, I was in a funeral home. That is very scary for me because I'm lucky to have all my loved ones still alive. I kept seeing members of my family around me, and I kept thinking, "Oh no, it's finally happened, somebody's gone." Everybody was crying, and the thing that was so frustrating was that I couldn't figure out who it was. I didn't see any pictures, and nobody would tell me who it was. So, I thought, "OK, let me go see where it (the coffin) is." I remember passing my family, and no one would talk to me because everyone was just inconsolable.

I went to the room and I got about halfway to the coffin when this arm just yanked me from behind. It gives me chills to talk about it. I turned around and it was the funeral director. She said, "No, I'm sorry, but visiting hours are over. You need to go home, you need to leave." I said, "But no, you don't understand, I just . . ."

She said, "No, no you need to leave now." I woke up very shortly after that and I was disturbed.

The next morning I woke up a little earlier than I normally do, so I left early for work. I was taking this road that's normally very busy, but because I left so early it wasn't. I was very tired. I was in the right hand lane and this moving truck, in what seemed like slow motion, came all the way over from the left hand side. It appeared the driver didn't even see me, and he was going to smash right into me. The only option I had was to slam my brakes, so I did. My car did a complete 180 and it spun out and faced oncoming traffic. If I would have left just a little bit sooner or later, I think something really bad could have happened. That road is normally really busy, and it was a miracle that there just happened to not be another car on the road when my car turned into the direction of traffic. Normally somebody would have hit me head on.

I think maybe the person who everybody was grieving for in the dream was possibly me! It kind of makes sense, because when I had the dream I remember that none of my family members were talking to me. I started to think that maybe it was because they couldn't see me, you know? Maybe it was because I was in the coffin. It gives me chills because it's exactly what I thought of as soon as I was safe. I wondered, "Wow, was that a warning?" That was very scary.

As you know, I shared another story on *Campfire* of a guardian angel who helped me when I was a little girl. I definitely, definitely believe that there's somebody looking out for me, I really do.

—*Elyse, Texas*

46
Tale of the Flying Shoes

I work at a large department store. My best friend and I had to do inventory in the shoe department bright and early at 5:30 a.m. The thing of it is that department is rumored to be haunted. There is a legend that a small child died there back in the sixties in the shoe department while running around, etc. I had become used to the idea that this place was haunted, so I didn't think about it much that morning.

It's a big, big warehouse and it's very tall so there's a twelve-foot ladder that you use to access the shoes. My friend and I were messing around, and we were sitting there eating breakfast just talking and chatting. Well, I looked up because I heard some shaking, and I know the reputation of this area being haunted.

More than twelve feet up, on the top shelf, I noticed one of the stacked shoe boxes start to move forward. I tried to tell myself that it was nothing, but I told my friend, "Hey, look at that." We were just both staring, and I asked him, "Dude, do you smell that?" He's like, "Yeah, it smells really bad." FYI, on some days you can smell bad urine in this department, like, really bad. In one particular corner, it can be overpowering.

Suddenly, all sixty or seventy pairs of shoes, every one of them, just flew off of the shelf. I screamed and dropped everything in my arms. Mind you, it's very early and the store wasn't open. There were maybe twenty people in this big store. I ran upstairs on an escalator, and I said I would not go back down there. The Owner thought I'd done this. She thought I was playing. She said, "Why did you do that?" I said, "I didn't do it, I swear I didn't do it. Check the camera, it wasn't us. We were not playing." She watched the video and she said, "It wasn't a rodent, there's no way a rodent could knock down all those shoes." To this day, I will not go down to the shoe department. I'm terrified of it. Others see stuff moving around, shoes moving around, and dark figures when they have to close the store at night. We don't get that many people working in the department for that very reason. They're so scared of it.

At the store, they won't tell us if the story about the girl is true. I tried to look it up. I asked a lot of the managers, and they say that they can't say anything. They're not supposed to talk about it.

—*Andrea, Texas*

47

An Angel of a Nurse

My grandfather was in the hospital for rotator cuff surgery. He had the procedure and he came out fine. Everything was dandy. My grandmother came to visit and he was telling her about this beautiful caregiver or nurse who came in to help him. He was talking about how nice she was and how her hair was so lovely. It was highly unusual for him, and it wasn't the way my grandfather would normally talk about women. Don't get me wrong, he loved women, but he wouldn't fawn over someone like that especially when they were only in his room for five minutes.

The next day, my grandmother came to pick up my grandfather and bring him home. The staff told her that they had lost him and she thought that they meant that they couldn't find him. She said, "Well, go get him." They said, "He passed away." This was all totally unexpected.

My grandmother thinks that lady my grandfather told her about was an angel visiting and she was preparing him to pass over.

—*Sarah, Pennsylvania*

48

Nuh Uh, Not Your Time

I had a Datsun Nissan 280ZX, it was a fall 1980-81 model and it was my very first car. I bought it off my boyfriend at the time, back in the '90s. When my boyfriend originally purchased it, the dealer told him that the driver's side seatbelt did not work. The locking mechanism was broken which was a little scary. So, being the third owner I was privy to that information,

My boyfriend and I had a fight one night, and I decided to go out for a drive. I was very upset, but I figured the drive would give me the time to go out and think. It was night time and I drove out to the Sedalia area because it's my Zen place. It's wonderful out there, but it's very dark at night on the back roads. As I came back around toward the highway, I came around a corner too fast and it was a dirt road. I skidded out, but I ended up going into the side of one of the foothills. It was stupid. I don't recommend driving at night when you are upset. The most interesting part of it was, as I started skidding out of control, someone shoved their hands into my chest, away from the front window, the windshield. For the very first time, the seat belt locked. It was as if somebody took that seat belt and jerked it tight.

I was physically alone. I ended up going up the side of the hill not into it. The way the car hit the side of the hill, the nose caught the hill so the tires went up. I was actually able to put the car in reverse, get back down on to the road, and drive to the gas station in Sedalia. There the car completely died. I called my boyfriend at one in the morning and said, "You need to come and get me." When I told him that the seatbelt locked, he did not believe it. We checked the seat belt afterward, and it didn't lock. In fact, the seat belt never worked again after that.

I believe I was protected that night, I really do. I've had an amazing life. My dad, my real dad, is a minister. He was an emergency room chaplain for twenty-three years and retired from hospice, so I've learned many things from him. He's an amazing human being, and yes, I do believe in miracles. That night my guardian angel said, "Nuh uh, not your time!"

I believe it was a spirit guide. I cannot equate it to one person. I just felt blessed. I realized I was given a second chance and I was never going to do that again.

—*Jana, Colorado*

49

Conversation with a Phantom

There's a place called the Uncountable Stones. It's in a little place called the Weald of Kent. It's historically thought to be the remains of an ancient, neolithic, burial mound. The legend has it that if you can count the stones, the Devil will come and grant your wish. Obviously, the wish that you are granted isn't necessarily what you expect it to be.

It's not going to be a good deal. If anyone has ever watched *Once Upon a Time,* you'll know that all magic comes with a price. Anyway, this place is also an area where a lot of Neo-Pagan rituals go on. During Midsummer's Eve and Midwinter's, they usually have quite a few things going on there.

A few years ago, I decided to go down there around midnight to watch what was going on. There's usually dancing, light torches, rituals, and things like that. I was sitting on one of these rocks, and I was speaking to this young lady. I was talking about the Uncountable Stones and saying how there's the story of a man, a farmer, who managed to count the stones by laying loaves of bread on the stones and knowing which ones that he counted and which ones he hadn't. I explained that he had a wish and it all went terribly wrong. She was very polite, very quiet, and very interested in what I had to say.

It was like we were talking for an hour or hour and a half. Then, the weirdest thing happened. I realized that everything had become very quiet. I was still talking to her, but I looked around and everything was dead. Everyone was gone including the girl, the place was quiet, and there wasn't a sound. I looked up. I couldn't see any stars. Everywhere around me was pitch black, and there was no one there. None of the candles, none of the torches were there, and neither were any of the people who were dancing and praying. It was just completely quiet.

I thought, "This is so weird. I must have fallen asleep." I stood up and checked my phone to see what time it was. The phone was completely dead. It was pitch black and I walked down this laneway. It was all covered with trees. It was very scary and very dark. All of a sudden, I saw this, almost like a . . . I don't know how to describe it. It was black. All I can say is that it was black and it came at me. Then, I was at the end of this laneway with these trees, right back to my car. I went to sit in my car. I looked at the time, and it was 3:30 a.m. To this day, I still have no idea what happened. I don't know what that black thing was, and I don't know who I was speaking with that evening. I don't know how everything changed the way it did.

I'm not sure what or who this woman was. There are many stories about mysterious women. Sometimes they are in the form of a hag, sometimes a banshee, and other times they are seen as a beautiful young woman who just appears there and talks to people. She doesn't harm them physically in any way, but she feeds on what they have to tell, and they experience all sorts of weird things, everything from blackouts to hallucinations. Seeing fairies, goblins, and all sorts of things like that. I'm the sort of person who looks for an explanation for everything. I keep thinking in the back of my mind, "I must have fallen asleep." Then I think to myself, "Surely someone would have woken me up when the festivities finished." I don't know.

Here is the weird thing. I don't know what she looked like. I can see her hair, but I can't visualize her face at all. I couldn't describe her in any way, except that I felt that she was a young woman. I wouldn't be able to describe what she looked like, what she sounded like, only that she was soft-spoken and quiet and seemed to be intensely interested in what I had to say.

I've been back there many times. Never in the middle of the night on Midsummer's Eve, but many times. It is quite close to another place called Kit's Coty with some other neolithic standing stones, which is also a very creepy place. I've never experienced anything like this before or since.

—Paul, United Kingdom

50
The Walking Pants

I grew up in the 90s with my younger sister. At the time that this event happened, my sister and I must have been about five and seven, respectively. We shared a room located at the end of a small hallway across from our parents' room. On the left and directly at the end of the hall was a big bookcase.

To set this up, I'll mention that my mom always wore these characteristic black jean leggings, which by modern standards are considered jeggings. Anyhow, one night we were lying in our beds. We were supposed to be sleeping, of course, but we were lying awake talking like kids do. All of a sudden, we both looked at the door because something caught our attention. I saw my mom's black jeggings, disembodied, run by and disappear into the bookcase. They looked as if someone was in them, like they were filled out, but you couldn't see any other part of the body. They were running and they were kind of suspended as if feet should have been there. They even made the sound of what it would sound like if legs were to rub against each other as they were running. There was no place for this thing to go because the end of the hall was right there. So my sister and I looked at each other, and I asked her, "What did you just see?" She described the exact same thing I had just seen. It was very bizarre. So I mustered up my courage and went downstairs to see if either of my parents had been upstairs recently. They both said no. In fact, my mom wasn't even wearing her jeggings at the time. To this day, that's been our little fun, little sisterly paranormal experience that we had together.

Regardless, my Mom couldn't believe our experience either. She thought it was incredible her pants just walked across the floor by themselves!

—*Alanna, New York City*

51

Fairy Fire

My next door neighbor invited my husband and I to join him and his wife for dinner at a local restaurant here in town. We went out for a lovely dinner and we returned home. My neighbors invited us to come in for coffee and dessert at their house after dinner. It was a very hot day in June, so we weren't in the mood for anything hot to drink. We had cake, ice water, and a great conversation. We decided to take our leave at about a quarter to nine. Since my husband works remotely, online, with a company on the East Coast, he had to get up very early the next morning.

It's only about 200 feet to our house, so we began our long "trek" back home. It was a pitch, moonless night. We live in a suburban, kind of rural area, and we couldn't see anything in front of us. Our neighbor offered to give us a flashlight, but I had a little one attached to my key chain and I thought it wasn't necessary to have another. Our friends' asphalt driveway is lit with solar lights, so we could find our way. On the other hand, our road is a dirt road. As soon as we got on the road, I heard a rustling beside me, on my right. On my left side, was a huge ranch with a cow pasture. The cows weren't around that week, so I didn't think it was a cow walking along with us. I was terrified by the sound, and when we stopped moving, the rustling also stopped. It seemed like something was walking alongside me. I used my little key chain flashlight and I didn't see a thing, so I was clinging to my husband for dear life. I was very terrified and he said, "You think that's scary? Why don't you look at the ground?" So, I did.

This is a dirt road, but what I saw was not what you'd expect. The ground was fluorescent green. Green, like a neon sign green. We were beside ourselves as we had never seen anything like this. We had no idea what it was. Both of us were extremely focused on walking straight and getting home. The green fluorescent rocks on the road continued to be green until we reached our house. The whole road was green. It was like we were following a fluorescent green road like the yellow brick road in The Wizard of Oz!

I would like to add that we had nothing to drink, no alcohol, none of us were drugged, nothing like that. The only thing we had to drink at dinner was a fruit iced tea and that was it. It was pomegranate iced tea, non-alcoholic, plus some water. That was it. We were not on any type of medications. So, when we approached our house we had a motion-detecting light that was always on very dimly, and as something approaches that light, it gets brighter. Well, for some reason the light was totally off. No one turned it off, it was on all the time, but the light did not work that evening. In fact, it never worked again after that night.

We were so glad to reach our house with no incident. We had no explanation as to what was rustling, walking around with us, and what caused the fluorescent green rocks on the road. We have friends who own a metaphysical shop in Bisbee, Arizona, and we happened to tell them what happened to us. They smiled and said, "You encountered Fairy Fire." We looked at each other, my husband and I, and asked, "What is Fairy Fire?"

Our friends went ahead and explained that it's an old Scottish folklore that fairies were some sort of beings, and they try to lure weary travelers by using this "Fairy Fire." They were trying to lure us into their dimension and their world by the sound of the rustling and by the fluorescent green rocks in the road. We were told if we would have stopped to pick up a rock or had gone ahead to investigate what the rustling was, we would have fallen into their dimension. Lucky for us, we were so focused on getting home that our energy overpowered theirs. That was the explanation.

I've never heard of it, but I did find the story of "Fairy Fire" online, and it is an old European folktale. It does lure weary travelers. Our metaphysical friends told us about an incident that happened to them that they describe as "Fairy Fire." They were visiting friends in New Mexico, and left. Then, they traveled a little bit down this road and they got hungry. They found a diner at about five in the morning, and it was bustling. There were cars outside, and they said it was strange that at five in the morning there would be so much activity at a diner. It was like a fifties-style diner, and they were struck by the fact that all the waiters, cooks, and customers were smoking. Yet, the food was wonderful, the service was great, and they said to themselves, "Next time we come back to visit, we're going to have another meal at this diner."

A couple years later, they went back to visit this friend again, and when they left, they decided that they were going to stop at this diner. They went down that road. There was no diner. They went a little further and they found a motel on the road, and they stopped and they asked where the diner was that they'd visited a couple years ago. The manager of the motel said there was never a diner there. There was never anything there on that same road. They feel that they fell into another dimension. Regardless, I have no explanation.

—Evelyn, Arizona

Jim Harold

52

The Ouija Strikes Again

This was back in the 1970s, and a couple of my high school girlfriends were at my house having a sleepover. We decided to be adventurous and play with a Ouija board. We planned to conjure up a dead person who had been very close to me and my family. He had been shot and killed. We asked the board, "Where is he? Can we speak to him?" The planchette just kept going to the "YES" repeatedly. That's all it would say. Then we moved on and my one girlfriend asked it when she was going to die. I did not like that and asked her to stop it.

I thought it was playing with fire, but sure enough it gave her a date. I don't remember the day, but I remember the month was February. We ended up spending most of the night up with that board. The next morning before school we were sitting with my mom at the breakfast table. She told us, "The awfullest thing happened to me last night." We all just looked at each other because we were all guilty about playing with the Ouija board. She said, "I woke up and somebody was pressing on my chest as hard as they could. In fact, the pressure was so bad I could feel their hands. I could hardly breathe." Let me tell you, talk about three teenagers looking at each other? It scared us to death. We thought, "What did we do?" We never told her what happened because we were afraid that we'd get in trouble for playing with it. She didn't even want Ouija boards in the house.

It didn't end there. We lived in a home that was built in the 1800s. That should have been our first clue not to play with the Ouija board. A week after this incident, I was asleep in my room, by myself, and I was awoken by my bed shaking. My bed was shaking so hard that it felt like my body was levitating. I was so scared. I've never been so frightened by anything in my life. So, I started praying. Well, it probably lasted maybe a minute or two, but it seemed like forever and then it just stopped. Everything got quiet. I got out of my bed, I ran downstairs, climbed into the middle of my parents' bed, and I wouldn't leave. I was so badly frightened. I told them what happened and they just chalked it up to a dream. Well, I didn't think I was dreaming, in fact, I know I wasn't.

I never had the bed shake anymore, but for a few years, I would have these episodes where my body felt like it was levitating. I would wake up and I felt like I was leaving my body. Years later, I learned about spontaneous Out of Body Experiences. When I look back, I honestly think that's what was happening to me, but I just didn't realize it at the time. I couldn't even talk about it for years, it scared me so badly. Did this have anything to do with the Ouija experimentation? I don't know, but you have to wonder.

Oh yes, there is one more thing. There definitely was something to that Ouija board that night. You might wonder what happened to that girl who had asked it when she would die? About ten years later, she died in a February car accident just as was predicted. It was so sad. When it happened it really made me think and what a horrible thing it was.

—*Brenda, Midwestern United States*

53

Playing in Traffic

We were living in New Jersey. I was riding in our car with my husband when the oddest thing happened. It was a normal, sunny day and we were in a bit of a traffic jam. Cars were backed up in both directions on the road where we were traveling. While we were sitting at a stop light, further down the road I noticed a man standing on the opposite side of the road on the curb.

Nothing unusual happened until the light changed and the traffic started to flow. The next thing I knew, this man stepped off the curb directly into traffic. I was completely stunned. I thought, "Oh my gosh, what's he thinking? What's he doing?" I couldn't believe my eyes. We were approaching the area where he stepped off. I completely expected to see a dead body lying in the street. Just as I looked over, I noticed that my husband had turned his head to look at something. I hadn't said anything about the man.

I asked him what he was looking at. He said, "I just saw this guy step out into the street." I told him I'd seen him as well. We're both looking and the strange thing was, no one slammed on their brakes and the guy didn't crouch down like he was going to jump into a car. Even if he had, the cars were moving where he stepped out into traffic. My husband and I were trying to make sense about what we had seen.

It was a head scratcher. He wasn't there and there was nobody lying on the street injured. When he stepped off the road, his posture was perfectly straight and tall. Had he been getting into a car, he would naturally duck down to crouch into it. He didn't do that. He stepped out like there was no traffic to be concerned about. We talked about it the whole way home and neither of us could really make sense of it. My husband said, "Well, maybe he jumped in the back of a truck." I didn't buy it because the man wasn't moving like that, he just stepped out straight into the road.

He went in between the vehicles that were blocking our view, so I just assumed he'd been hit or he got into a car. Looking back on it, he couldn't have possibly gotten into a car. If I'd just seen it myself, it might not have made the same impression on me, but my husband saw it as well. That day we fully expected to see blood or a body lying on the ground, but there was nothing. The common sense thing seems that it had to be a ghost or a time slip, I don't know. It was strange.

—*Jane, South Carolina*

54

A Strange Commute

About a year and a half ago, I was going into work, which is about a thirty-, maybe forty-five-minute commute on a bad day. I had been making the same trek on the highway from city to city for three and a half years. For some reason, one day when I came in my boss looked at me and said, "Martin, I thought you weren't coming in today." I said, "What do you mean?" She said, "Well, you're an hour and a half late." I said, "No, it's eight o'clock." She said, "No, it's nine thirty."

I looked at her, confused. I looked at the clock on the computer, and sure enough, she was right. It was 9:30 am! Now, there was no traffic on the road, it was a perfectly clear day, and somehow a half hour turned into an hour and a half. The thing that was kind of weird, compared to other missing time things that I've heard about was that nothing else happened. I didn't get sucker-punched by Bigfoot or abducted by aliens. That was the thing. I just drove to work as I always do, left at the same time, and there was nothing unusual.

I left at a quarter past seven, the same time I leave every single day. Like I said, I only take one highway into work. In Michigan, we do seventy mph on our highways, so truth be told, I go more like seventy-five. If I were to be an hour and a half late, I'd have had to be doing twenty to twenty-five mph the entire time.

Just in case anyone out there is thinking this, it was past daylight savings. We already did the spring forward. It was just a normal Wednesday. There was nothing amazing about it at all except for this missing time.

I have no theories as to what happened. When I got there, I just kind of said to myself, "I know what this is, but I'm not going to think about it." I went about my day and left it alone. Never even told my wife until today.

Maybe my boss just assumed I was BSing. She said, "Whatever, you've got vacation time. Use it." She didn't really ask me any questions and I wasn't like, "Oh God, missing time phenomenon, where was I?" I just kind of shrugged my shoulders and said, "OK, sure." I signed out and left the office.

I kind of already had the reputation as "that guy" in the office, the one that likes Bigfoot and stuff, so it was best to just not touch it.

—*Martin, Michigan*

Jim Harold

55

I Had a Teenage Doppelgänger

There were two separate incidents when this occurred. The first was when I was around nineteen years old. I was attending community college and my mom and I had an argument the night before. It was a pretty heated argument and we were yelling at one another. I never did that with my mom, but at this point there was just a lot of tension in the house.

It got so bad that my mom said, "You know what, Lisa? Tomorrow morning, when you get ready to go to school, don't even come in here and tell me goodbye in the morning because I'm so mad at you right now. I don't even want to look at you." I said, "Fine, I'm not going to come in and talk to you then. I'm just going to go to school." The next morning I had set my alarm clock and off to school I went.

Being in college, I was done at 12:30 p.m. and I had just gotten back home and everything had cooled down. My mom said.

"Oh, you thought you were smart this morning." I said, "What are you talking about?" She goes, "I saw you looking in at me this morning." I said, "Mom, I never even came into your room this morning." She said, "Lisa, you thought I was sleeping but I watched you open the door at look in at me." I said, "Mom, honest to God I wasn't in there, I never went into your room." She said, "You thought you could even be smarter, when I came out of the bedroom, I watched you walk past the doorway. I looked up at you, you turned, you had on that purple coat."

She was talking about a purple coat that I had at the time. She said, "I looked right at you, you had your coat on this morning. You looked right at me, and turned your head and kept walking." She was put off by that and said, "I thought to myself, 'Well, hmm. I'm not talking to her either.'" I said, "Mom, honest to God, I wasn't there. I never saw you this morning. What time was this?" She said, "I guess it was around nine thirty." I said, "Mom, I was in my psychology class at nine thirty." There was nobody there. I don't have brothers or sisters, so there couldn't have been a mistaken identity at that point. My mom believes me because she experienced so much in the home as well.

I didn't even know what a doppelgänger was until I was sharing this with a psychic and she explained the concept to me. The second story is short and not as creepy. I was sitting in the family room, and I could see my mom in the kitchen. I saw her walk into the kitchen and I figured she must have been over by the stove. I could hear her cutting something like cheese or pepperoni and I hollered out to her, "What are you doing?" She didn't answer me. I went back to the TV and I could still hear this so I was wondering what in the heck was she cutting. I wanted a little bit of whatever she had. When I went out to the kitchen there was nobody there. I hollered, "Mom! Mom!"

She said, "I'm in the back bedroom." I went back and asked, "What were you cutting out in the kitchen?" She said, "What are you talking about?" I knew it was one of those things again, because when I found my mother, she was sitting in the middle of the bed. She had about four dresser drawers out around her. She was cleaning out and rearranging her drawers and she was sitting in the center of it. There was no way that she could have been out in that kitchen, cutting whatever it was, eating it, and then back within the bedroom in two minutes.

We did develop a theory. We researched the home and went to an event with Lorraine and Ed Warren. We attended a seminar at Chatham College and at the end of the seminar everybody told their spooky story. My mom was hesitant about it but felt we needed help, and we needed to find something out. I raised my hand and I started telling them the story and stayed after the seminar. The Warrens both came out to the home the following day.

They believed that at one time there was an eleven room farmhouse built on the property and there was a little girl who was five-years-old by the name of Claire. There was a man, we don't know if he was the father of this child or a boyfriend to the mother and his name was John. There was a woman who was the mother of the little girl, her name was Elsie. From what we gathered, he was not very kind to this little girl and was doing terrible things to her. He told her basically that if you tell, I'm going to kill you and then kill your mother. Well, it turns out that the little girl did tell and the man did kill the little girl. The mother ended up killing him with an ax in the area of our kitchen, and then she hung herself. It wasn't in the actual home that we live in, it was where the house now stands.

The way that the home was acquired was very mysterious as

well. The lady of the house couldn't wait to get out of there. She said she was relocating because of her husband's job in another state. After talking to the neighbors who we've lived next to for thirty years, we learned the real story. The wife would come running to their house during the day and said that there were people walking in the home, people were talking to her, and that she could hear them. When they moved, it was only maybe twelve miles from the house. They never moved out of state. There's just so many other things that happened, but we'll save that for another time . . .

—*Lisa, Pennsylvania*

Jim Harold

56
Strange Little Lights

This is a really short story, but I think it is really unique. I was about ten or eleven years old. I shared a room with my older brother who was about three years older than me. The house itself was a back split. You call it a split level in the States. From the highest floor, when you're on the landing, there's only about five or six steps down and you can see the dining room/living room area. You have a pretty clear view.

On this occasion, I woke up in the middle of the night. I just couldn't sleep. Often, I would just walk to the bathroom across the landing, go into the bathroom, pour myself a cup of water and go back to bed. This night I did that. Then, I walked around my brother's bed and walked outside the room.

I recall just looking down, and seeing tons and tons of little red lights. Right now, the only thing I could say that they look like were LED lights, which weren't even on the consumer market at the time. It was very dark and they were scurrying across the floor, but they weren't randomly scurrying like insects. They were going in a horizontal fashion, left to right across the floor of the landing downstairs. I recall staring at these for a few seconds. There must have been about thirty or forty of them.

I faintly recall that they were spaced out equally and going left to right and it was really weird. I can't recall if there was noise associated with them or not. I just remember that I ran right back into my bedroom. I tried to wake up my brother. He kind of woke up and being an older brother, he was just dismissive. I told him that there were these lights downstairs and he still wouldn't bother to get up. I don't know what it was, but in my mind I thought they were robots. They seemed mechanical, not organic, if you know what I mean?

The lights weren't high up. They were just a few inches off the floor. So whether they were small insects or what, I don't know. I thought they were robots, but it seems silly saying that.

It's so hard to say now what it was, because it was so long ago. At the time, I believed that I actually saw something. Thinking as an adult, my logical brain wants to kick in and say that it must have been a dream or a hallucination, or there were lights coming in from outside, but I can't imagine what would have caused that kind of thing.

It was a strange experience, and it almost left my memory. It didn't come back until a couple of years ago when I actually started listening to your show. I was thinking, "Well, nothing paranormal has ever happened to me." Then, I remembered this incident and how bizarre it was.

—*Robert, Canada*

57

Queen of the Dragonflies

I was about nine or ten-years-old visiting my grandparent's farm in western Pennsylvania when this story took place. They had this beautiful farm, and about 100 feet back from the house there was this gorgeous little stream that had willow trees. To the right of the willow trees, my grandfather had dammed this stream up and made a little heart-shaped pond.

We were there to have dinner with my grandparents so my little brother and I decided to kill some time. Since we weren't allowed to stray too far from the house we decided we'd just go meander out back and walk along the water. I kind of hopped the stream at one point where it wasn't very wide. My little brother was on one side of the pond and I was on the other side. We were just looking at the minnows, tadpoles and everything. I think it was early fall, because the willow trees were starting to lose their leaves.

The house was landscaped, and aside from those willow trees, my grandfather had totally cleared the land. There was a lawn that was perfectly manicured. In other words, there was no tall grass or anything like that. Anyhow, we were just kind of standing there and out of the corner of my eye on the left hand side zoomed in this massive bug. I mean, we're watching the dragonflies and damselflies flit about, but this bug was beyond anything I had ever seen.

I'll describe it to you. The head seriously, this is going to sound kind of crazy even for me, but the head was about the size of a softball. The body kind of just came out of the head, and the body was anywhere from twelve to eighteen inches long. It had four wings like a dragonfly, but the coloration was more like a yellow jacket, where it had clearly defined yellow and black stripes. The head was yellow, and because from where I was standing the sun was behind me, I could see the sun shining off this, so it was a really shiny exoskeleton, so to speak.

Anyway, this thing came buzzing out. My brother's eyes were as big as saucers and his mouth was wide open. I asked, "Do you see this?" He just kind of nodded and said yes. I said, "Is it a toy? What is this thing?" He just said, "I don't know." We both started looking around for somebody flying this thing. We were stumped because it really didn't look like anything we'd ever seen.

I'm old, so back in the day the only thing that you did radio control with were those gasoline-powered airplanes. The ones that would take you six months to build and you'd break it like within five minutes of getting it off the ground. Plus, they were really noisy. Of course, as I just said, except for the willow trees, it was a total clearing, so there was no one or nothing there. No one could have been hiding anywhere. I watched it around the pond and it was buzzing. In school, I had just studied bugs, so I knew that every bug has a head, a thorax, and an abdomen. But the anatomy on this one was strange, either the thorax was really thick or it straight went down into a tail. You know how a dragonfly kind of has that beautiful shape? This bug just kind of went straight down. It was very odd. It had six legs and antennae. I watched it come around the pond. It's a pretty small pond. The bug came around me again and I looked at it wondering, "Wow, what is this thing?" I kept thinking about it being something prehistoric almost. Then, I dubbed it the "queen of the dragonflies." It had four wings, even though she didn't really look like a dragonfly except for that, that's where my nine-year-old mind went.

Another thing that was strange was that it was quiet. When it would go past, the wings would almost make a little bit of a whoosh, because they were big, but there was no sound. It took the same path as a dragonfly or a damselfly, just the inner lip of the pond. I decided that if it was going to dive bomb me, I was going to be on the other side of the pond so I could run to the house. On the second round, I jumped over the stream and beside my little brother, about six feet away. We were both watching and we were about to run. It came towards me, coming around the pond again, and it just stopped and hovered in front of my face! You know how sometimes a hummingbird or a bee will think that you're a big flower, and kind of checks you out? It was that kind of a thing. It was about two and a half, maybe three feet away. Maybe for a moment, it thought I was supper.

I can't remember exactly what the mouth was like, but I don't think it had, for your bug people, a mandible thing. The wings were clearly at least two and a half feet. I mean, they were way past my shoulders.

This bug hovered in front of me, probably just for a second or two, but it seemed like a long time. I started to think if this thing had a stinger it was bad news, because if it's like a mosquito and it sucks your blood, you're going to be a quart down. It kind of veered back and it went off again. I asked my little brother, "What is that thing?" He looked at me and he was as white as a sheet. He just said, "I don't know." When I turned to look back for it, it was gone. Vanished.

We were frantically looking for it because we didn't want this thing behind us. We were in a big clearing except the willow trees, which frankly I don't think it could have flown through because with its wing span it would have got caught in the branches. You could have seen this thing from a long way off because it was yellow and black striped. It was very clearly marked. It kind of disappeared from the same spot it appeared from, which was the mouth of the dam. Really weird. We started to walk back to the house and the whole time we were dumbfounded. My brother was visibly shaken, and I was thinking of how could we have caught that thing. I was thinking we'd need a really big net. I said, "I want to go back and try to catch it." It was funny because for me because I was only nine or ten. I didn't think of it as anything paranormal. I just thought of it as something I'd just never seen before. It's just like if you put a wombat in front of me, I wouldn't know what that was either, but I would have believed it because it was right in front of me. To me it was just a bug I'd never seen before. I was all about trying to catch this thing.

Years later, my little brother and I would talk about it, and we would say, "Remember that big bug down at the pond? What was that thing?" Then, after we hit a certain age, we just never talked about it anymore. Life happens. Well, for some strange reason last year, the memory came back to me. You know how sometimes you're not thinking of anything and something comes back from your past? I said, "Oh my God, that bug, I've got to tell Jim that story! And this is a good one, because my little brother was there and he can verify it."

So I was all about trying to get him to describe what he saw to me, so I'd know that I wasn't totally insanely crazy. Last Christmas, I was at his house and I kept thinking in my head, "There's something I want to ask him, there's something I want to ask him. Oh yeah, the bug!" So I said, "Hey Jack, do you remember that time that we were down by the pond and there was that bug?" He said, "I don't remember that. I don't know what you're talking about." I started to describe it a little bit, because I was really trying to get him to remember it himself but I didn't want to put anything in his head. He said, "Nope, I don't like bugs. I don't want to talk about it."

I was like, what? I've never known my brother to be afraid of anything. I've never known him to be afraid of bugs. At first, I really thought he was just pulling my leg. I said, "OK. No, you remember it. Here, let me sketch it out for you." He said, "No, I'm not even going to look at it. Don't even bother drawing it, I'm not going to look at it," I said, "Come on, come on." I was laughing because I'm obnoxious like that. I drew it out and I slid it towards him. He slapped his hand over it and shot it back at me and said, "I'm not even going to look at that. Bugs freak me out. They creep me out."

I thought, maybe he got a phobia? He was clearly really scared, and I'm wondering if that was his trigger. For me, it was the total opposite effect. It made me get into bugs. I remember going home and looking at encyclopedias. I was trying to look at bugs and to see if I could try to find that shape, so I could see what species it belonged to. Of course, I never could.

Before I told you this story, I took a look on the Internet and I haven't seen anything like this. I mean, I never heard, in all *The Paranormal Podcast* shows, *In Search of . . .* episodes, and books I've read, I have never heard of anybody talk about a cryptid insect. It's always been Bigfoot or a chupacabra, and I can't be the only person who has experienced this. I don't even know what to say about it. I know this sounds really crazy, but I could draw that thing right now. I mean, the way his eyes looked when he faced me, the markings. He had these beautiful symmetrical black markings on his yellow exoskeleton, and antennae. I would like to be hypnotically regressed, and get my brother and I to both go back to see. I want to really verify it.

I've never heard anybody even talk about something other-worldly that was insect-like. The fact that it appeared and disappeared the way it did, it was like it came out of another dimension, like Bigfoot, you know what I'm saying? I looked at my little brother and turned back, and it was gone. Where we were standing, we had a great vantage point and could see for acres. As big as that thing was, we would have seen it even at a distance. I have a lot of stories, but this has been the biggest stumper I've ever experienced in my life.

—*Sandy, California*

PART FOUR

PETS
AND THE
SUPERNATURAL

58

Wanna Play Ball

work nights and my wife works days. On this night she happened to be going to bed about the time I was getting ready to jump into the shower. We were standing there and I was giving her a kiss. We were exchanging a few words about our day and we just happened to hear something kind of odd in our living room. We looked in the direction of where we thought it was coming from and we saw our female husky, Kia, at her water bowl getting a drink. All of a sudden, her yellow tennis ball comes flying over her head! I said, "She wasn't playing with that. She was getting water." Then, I looked around to see if any of my other dogs just happened to be jumping up and playing with the ball. They were all sound asleep!

My wife and I were standing there, kind of puzzled, wondering how in the world did this happen? The ball literally moved itself? Nobody touched it and no animal touched it. It literally moved over the dog's head independently.

There was no one else in the house and the ball went over her head by about five or six inches. I've seen videos of balls moving, but never one flying over my dog. My wife has never been a big believer in the paranormal, so she just kind of looked to me and said, "What was that?" I just joked, "Oh, it's a ghost in the house." She said, "OK, whatever." To this day we don't know what happened, but we both saw it.

Strange things happen in this house. More than once I've been in bed talking to who I thought was my wife. I could feel someone in the bed. When I looked I could see an imprint where somebody was sitting on the bed, but there was no one there. It was like an invisible person was sitting there! Then, the mattress kind of raised up as if somebody were getting off of it.

My wife bought the house about four years before we got married. The lady who owned it before passed away, but I don't know if it was in the house or not. It was built to her specifications since she was in a wheelchair. Her sister lives across the street and is very nice. I just figure that this woman is coming back to visit every now and again. I can't blame her as it's a nice little house. Nothing has ever been mean or malicious. One of my daughters had an "old hag" experience that kind of startled her. She said, "I just woke up and someone was staring at me." She said it was "an old woman with wiry hair." She had the paralysis part that goes along with the old hag syndrome and that is what really frightened her. The lady didn't look mean or anything like that.

I think this woman is just still wandering around here checking up and making sure I'm taking care of the place. Between her and my wife, I don't have any choice but to hold up my end of the bargain. We have four daughters and five dogs, so I know where I rank and it's just above the huskies!

—*Scott, Kentucky*

59

Rainbow Bridge Reunion

I am a single person and live alone so my dogs are my children. 2010 was not a good year for me. My grandmother from my mom's side of the family was very slowly passing away, and so it was a pretty tough year. I started off the year with two fifteen-year-old dogs and their troubles started in January. Muffy, my little miniature poodle, started developing a heart problem, having seizures, and I ended up having to help her cross the Rainbow Bridge. Then, my border collie mix was just broken-hearted over the loss of her best friend. Both of them had been rescue dogs. Nothing I did would pull her out of the slump that she was in. She just basically grieved herself away. During Memorial Day weekend, I had to help her across the Rainbow Bridge too. I came home and I just left her collar with her tags in the car. I just didn't want to deal with it. I came into the house and for the first time in fifteen years I walked into an empty house. I just fell apart. I just fell down on the couch and had a Scarlett O'Hara moment. I completely lost control.

I got up and went to wash my face. I heard Muffy, who had passed away in January. I had her ashes and collar sitting on top of the box with her ashes on a very large and very deep window sill. It had been sitting there since January and it had not moved. Then all of a sudden I heard Sophie too, who was the dog I had just had to help across that day. I heard her tags.

They were distinctive sounds and both dog's tags sounded different. I heard Sophie's tags, and they were in the car in the garage, not even in the house. Then I heard Muffy's tags, the one that had passed away in January. I dried my face, walked into the living room, and Muffy's tags were swinging on her box. I didn't have a ceiling fan on or anything like that, but yet they were actually moving. I thought, "Oh, Sophie found Muffy." That's how I felt, and that's what I think happened. They were both letting me know that they were together again.

—*Julie, Oklahoma*

60

Just Once, Mommy

It was about 1995 and I was living in Illinois. I was recently divorced and living alone except for my two dogs. I wasn't earning a lot of money and things were very tight. I was very blue this night.

At the time, I had a high-strung dachshund and he was a freak for playing fetch. He'd play it all day. If you had somebody throwing it, he would go. When we went down to my parent's house, there would be somebody there throwing a ball all day. I've literally seen him falling asleep sitting up and being sore the next day. He would just go until he couldn't go anymore.

I came home that evening and sat on the couch. He was there and he was all happy. He put the ball beside me on the couch and I looked down at him. I said, "Give me a break, will you?" I talk to my dog out loud. I heard in my head a little kid's voice, not like a small child, but a voice of a child of four or five. One that could speak well, but was still young. I heard in my head, "Just once, Mommy? Please?"

I looked down at him and I said out loud, "I didn't just hear that." I looked at the ball beside me and I thought, "Well, there's just one way I can find out because I know if I throw this ball once, I'm going to be throwing it all night." So I took the ball and I threw it. He ran, he played and I waited. That dog never brought the ball back to me that whole night, not once.

There was some kind of telepathy going on, where the dog said "just once" and he stood by it. He kept his word. That was extremely out of character for him, because that wasn't his personality at all.

—*Diana, Arizona*

61

Riding the Storm from Beyond

This happened in late August 2005. The reason I know the date is because it was when Hurricane Katrina was trekking across Alabama. This particular night it was storming really badly. I live in a tiny little house by myself, so naturally it was frightening.

I had moved in about six months prior and had both of my dogs with me at the time. After a week there, my first dog died. He had been very sick. Three months later, the other one died. I was completely alone in this house with Katrina barreling right toward me.

The storm was awful and I couldn't sleep. When I'd look through the window at the trees outside, I fully expected them to fall on the house. There was a lot of lightning and the wind felt as though it was going to blow the house off the hill. I was lying in bed and watching the shadows of the lightning reflecting off the ceiling, when I felt the bed start to vibrate.

I was just lying there, thinking how strange all of this was. I didn't know what to do other than just ride it out. My bed continued to vibrate and it felt like it raised off the floor at the foot and the sensation gradually started to move up the bed. This vibration was moving its way up the bed and I was freaking out, but I could feel Roddy, my dog, next to me. I thought, "Well, he's not upset. He's really calm and if he's not upset, I'm OK."

I was so flustered by the storm that I wasn't recalling that Roddy had died and that he couldn't be there. The vibration continued all the way until it got to the head of the bed, and it just stopped.

You can tell me I was dreaming, but I have insomnia and I couldn't have dreamt in the middle of a storm like that. All I can think of is that Roddy, my dog, was telling me goodbye with his last bit of energy. I've thought about it a lot, and that's the only explanation I can come up with to explain that night.

—*Patti, Alabama*

PART FIVE

UFOs

62

Eagle
Dancer

*Note From Jim: What fascinates me about this short
story is that we've had similar reports from other
listeners and others that originate from the American
Southwest. It makes one wonder what is going on.*

I am of Native American heritage and to set this up, I should
explain what an Eagle Dancer is. An Eagle Dancer is a traditional native dancer with a full headdress and costume. You
can't call it a costume. It is like a uniform with eagle feathers,
head gear, turquoise beads on his chest, wearing like a skirt.

This was 1966 when I was about ten years old. My family was
going out to New Mexico to visit my cousins and relatives and I
was lying down in the back of the car. I remember that I woke up
and it was a beautiful day. I looked up at the sky and there was

an Eagle Dancer, perfectly detailed as a cloud. You could see the head, the beads, everything. His wings were expanded outwards and you could see his head and a beak.

I was astounded and mesmerized by it. I begged my dad, "Stop, let's take a picture of this cloud." It was so perfect. He said, "We're not allowed to do that."

We couldn't stop. I had a little thirty-five-millimeter film camera, and I wanted a picture of this thing so badly. The detail was so perfect. To this day, I've not seen a cloud like that. You could see the feathers, and the head. It was like taking a snow figure and carving it perfectly. I'm in my fifties now, but when you're a young kid and you see something cool and impressive, it always remains with you for a long time.

—Myron, *Ohio*

63
A UFO
Déjà Vu

I have two UFO experiences I'd like to share. Though it is out of sequence, I'll share the most dramatic first.

The strangest experience I have ever had occurred in 1994. I was about fifteen years old. We'd just finished eating dinner at a Chinese restaurant with my family, and we were on our way home. We lived in the country, so on the way back I was looking out of the window. On our left hand side, I saw this strange light up in the sky. There were some hills on the road, and as we reached the top of one and started going down the hill, I could see there was something in the sky sitting right about at treetop level.

I caught the attention of my family and said, "Look out the window." Everyone looked, and my father stopped the car immediately. There was a triangle UFO floating right above the treetops and a pond that was there. The UFO was probably about the size of a football field. It had a white light on each corner. The funny thing about this was this was not the first time that I'd seen something like this.

The UFO was completely black, and like I said, it had a white light on each corner. My mom was hysterical, absolutely terrified. My brother and I were stunned, but we got out of the car anyway. My dad said that he would leave us there, take my mother back home, which wasn't that far away, get a camera, and return. So, they went home. My brother and I stayed behind sitting there watching this thing. I remember that it had to be summertime, because you could hear the frogs and crickets, but the UFO made no noise at all. It just floated there. Like I said, it was about tree height, maybe 100 feet high, so it was really visible. My brother and I sat there for a couple of minutes looking at this thing, and we got really afraid So, we started running up the road towards our house. As you went down one hill, you had to go back up another hill to get back to our home. As we ran up the hill, the craft started following us. We started getting really scared at that point. My father had dropped my mother off, and was headed back down to where he left us. My brother and I had gotten only about 300 yards away from our house, when Dad came speeding down the driveway. He pulled up right to where my brother and I were standing in the middle of the road. Just as he got there, the craft took off at a fairly high speed and headed back over the tree tops. We saw its direction, which must have been westerly, and we got in the car with my father. He had a camera and we spent the next forty-five minutes to an hour chasing this object, hoping it would become stationary again so we could get a good picture but it never did.

As I mentioned, this wasn't the first time I saw something like this. When I was I was about five or six-years-old, we lived in a small town in called Sanford, North Carolina. I was awoken one night at about three in the morning. We lived right next to Fort Bragg. My brother and I used to see jets flying over the tree tops, and when we heard the jets flying, we would run out to see them. They flew so low you could almost read the bottom wing markings on them. I guess they were doing low-flying radar evasion exercises or something like that. Anyway, this one night I was awoken by a loud rumbling sound, and I looked out the window. We lived on a big hill, so my window sat pretty much right at tree level. I looked out of the window, and I saw the point of a triangle. This time it was not a white light, but actually a purple light on the corner of the triangle, and it was not just sitting stationary, but rotating very slowly. I watched it spin for a minute or two, and then I ran into my parents' room and woke them up. They came into my bedroom, and they saw it go back over the back of our yard, over the tree tops. They got a short glimpse of it, and that was the first time I'd actually seen one of those before. There were some similarities between both experiences, but some differences too. Both times it was black, but the first time it was making a rumbling noise. The second time there was no noise at all. Regardless, this is something that the whole family experienced. It's not something they really talk about often, but they will acknowledge the fact. They're more afraid of it than anything else. They really don't want to speak about it, it's a taboo kind of thing. As you reach back further in the generations, there is a reluctance to talk about these things.

You asked if I thought I'd been abducted and it is something I think about. There was another incident that involved my wife and I. Originally, I thought this was a dream, but I'm not quite sure anymore. The power went out at our house and it is very hot here in the summertime since we live in the South. My parents were out of town when this happened, so we went to stay at their house to take advantage of their air conditioning to keep cool. This happened probably somewhere around ten or eleven at night. We hadn't been there long, but we went downstairs and pulled the couch out in the downstairs' living room and laid down. Since I was asleep, I'm telling the story second hand, but my wife says we were lying there and all of a sudden, she saw this bright flash of light outside of the windows. She heard this rumbling, and it shook the entire house. She said there was light shining into the house like it was daytime. She became hysterical and was trying to wake me, but I would not wake up. That is very unusual for me because I'm a very light sleeper. All of a sudden, she was asleep and woke up the next morning. I can't deny that there have been some very strange experiences that I've encountered in my lifetime.

To be quite honest I was very nervous when you first called. It's been something I've never really talked about it with anybody, I've told the story to a couple of my friends, but not a whole lot of people. I do believe that there is probably something to it, but I can't say for sure and to be quite honest with you I really don't want to know.

—*Chris, South Carolina*

64
The Dancing Lights

This happened about fifteen or sixteen years ago. I was up in Maine visiting my sister who has a little farm in the central portion of the state. I brought my tent and I camped out away from the house. I wanted to be by myself.

It was nighttime and I had a good fire going. It was a beautiful starry night, everything was crystal clear and you could see the Milky Way very clearly. It looked like there were about a billion stars in the sky. I was just stargazing and sitting around the fire. I could see satellites traversing the sky occasionally. There were distant planes, things like that but nothing unusual.

Finally, I got tired and retired to my tent. Not two minutes after lying down, a light appeared on the roof of the tent. It was about four inches in diameter. It was like somebody shining a flashlight down on it, but it would skip around from point to point, disappearing in one spot and reappearing in another. It did that for about three minutes. It looked like it was scanning something. I know that no one was playing a joke on me because logistically someone couldn't reach up that high over the tent with a flashlight. I was 100 yards from the house and I didn't hear anything. There was no noise. It was completely silent.

After a couple minutes of watching this, I was mesmerized. I don't know why I didn't go outside during all of this to look and see what was doing this. A few minutes after it stopped, I thought, "What the hell?" I opened the tent, ran out and I looked up. All I could see were the stars, nothing else. I was camped in a clearing. I looked around and there was nothing around me. There was nobody, no noise, no nothing. I was pretty excited, so I couldn't sleep. I just threw some more wood on the fire. I stayed up for another hour or so, but nothing else happened. It was just that one experience.

The whole thing was pretty strange. I don't know how to explain it. I think it could have been some kind of space ship or something up there. It was silent and shining a light on my tent. That's exactly what happened. I can't explain it, and I can't say that I saw a craft or anything. The light was real and it was dancing around on the top of my tent.

It's totally out of the question that it was anything with a motor or anything like that. At least it wasn't any kind that we would understand. Someone might say that they were lasers, but they weren't. Lasers are a point of light, but as I said, this was approximately four inches in diameter, like the size of a flashlight beam or a little larger.

I kick myself to this day for not immediately going out there and looking up while it was scanning or doing whatever it was doing. I couldn't. I was just frozen in the tent watching it. I really wonder if anyone else has ever experienced anything similar to this. It is wild to think something or someone was interested in my little tent from so far away.

—Joe, Maine

65

A Mystery
in the Deadwood Skies

I was fortunate enough to be a child musician. I was home schooled and grew up traveling all over the United States. At the time this story takes place, I was living near Deadwood, South Dakota. My dad and I both were classical flamenco guitarists, and we were playing at a little Mexican restaurant. It was located in a town called Spearfish. We were living in a beautiful, large home outside of Deadwood.

One night, we were traveling through Deadwood and there are entire, hundreds of miles of area through the Black Hills where there are no streetlights. Other than the homes, at night headlights are the only source of light when you are on the road. My parents were in the front seat with my dad driving. My best friend and I were in the back. We're traveling back from this nightclub and it was about eleven thirty at night. Both my friend and I were nine years old at the time. He and I were chatting while my mom and dad were talking to each other up in the front. My dad started playing with the lights, saying, "Look how dark it is." He'd turn off the lights and, of course, that would scare my mom. So she would say, "Art, turn those lights back on!" He would comply. He would play with the high beams, flash them, and he was just fooling around.

Around the bend, we saw lights flash back at us. So my dad, figuring somebody in another car was in a playful spirit, flashed his lights again. We were in an old Cadillac so he just tripped the light switch back and forth a couple of times. Then he said, "Oh, maybe somebody's on the side of the road or maybe somebody's trying to alert me of something." We saw something on the berm, off the side of the road, so we pulled over. At first viewing it from the car, this object looked like it might have been an overturned vehicle, just some metal structure. As we got closer it turned out to be fairly large. It looked like a stainless steel ice cream cone turned upside down.

The wider part was on the bottom, coming to a small maybe two or three foot section on top. It had a light that was sweeping around the road and the woods in a large wide circle. I clearly remember it having something like radio aerials, but they were flexible. These aerials were whipping around, making a sound kind of like a jump rope.

We all just watched this big light for a moment, and then my mom said, "Art, get us the bleep out of here." My dad hit the gas and we took off. My mom told us, "Nobody say anything until we get home." We drove another ten miles or so to get to our home, which was in Brownsville, right outside Deadwood. She said, "Everybody take a piece of paper and draw what you saw." We did. I still have the pieces of paper somewhere in my stuff. We all saw the same thing.

My mom called the authorities. I don't know which ones, since she's no longer with us, but it must have been on the next day. We had two guys that came and took our report. Even as a kid, I remember thinking that we really must have seen something important.

The story doesn't end there. That same year my friend and I were wandering the Black Hills woods behind my house, and we came across what looked like slaughtered cattle. We showed my mother. Some of them were strangely . . . well, I found out later they were what they call cattle mutilations.

We had a farmer next door to us. We got him and he walked back around with us and he said, "These are not my marks." He had no idea how they got there and didn't recognize the brand on them. He didn't recognize anything. There must have been four or five of these cattle over time. It was just very strange. I don't know if it was not from this world or something, but I always thought maybe it was a governmental thing? I don't know, but has stuck with me my whole life. I have looked for similar versions of this story from MUFON (Mutual UFO Network) and lots of places, but it's a really unique one.

My dad is now seventy-three. We both recently sat down and had a beer with my best friend. We recounted the story. Even after all these years, we have pretty similar recollections. There are a few differences. My father doesn't remember the aerial things whipping around, but I very clearly do. I think he thought it was a little different size, but considering this was 1979, our recollections are pretty similar. That night in the Black Hills definitely had a lifelong impact on us.

—Lucien, Massachusetts

66

UFO Rendezvous

This was in the 1990s when I lived in Ohio. I worked at a place in Columbus which is basically in the center of the state. I worked second shift, so I was getting off work eleven thirty or midnight. For about three or four weeks, myself and three of my coworkers and I saw three different lights that kind of flew around in set patterns. We thought it was strange.

I decided on the way home one summer night that I was just going to try to find out what these lights were. As I was traveling home, I was headed west from Columbus in the direction of where these lights had been appearing. Looking out of my windshield, there were three lights. One of them was on the left side of my field of vision. It would start about halfway up from the horizon, it would slowly travel down, loop up, go back up, then loop down and come back down.

It kept repeating that kind of pattern. The second light started on the right side of the horizon and then slowly went across to the left, kind of looped back up a little bit, and then it sort of disappeared. About a second and a half later, it reappeared on the right side of the horizon. That was the pattern of the second light. The third light was on the right side of my field of vision. It was doing the up and down pattern just like the light on the left side.

For some reason, I decided that I was going to try to figure out what these lights were, so I decided that on my way home I was going to flash my headlights on high beam every time I turned toward the direction of these lights. About thirty minutes into my drive, I was about ten minutes from home. Once the light on the right side reached the top of its travel and would start to come down, it would start to get bigger. I took that to mean that it was coming towards me. So, I decided that I was going to pull off on a little access road to this farm, and I was going to sit there with my bright lights on.

I sat there and this light got bigger and bigger. I started to notice that it had a shape to it and I got out of the car to watch this whatever this was come toward me. I didn't really have a good frame of reference because there wasn't anything around me, it was just an open field, but this thing looked to be about thirty or forty feet long. It was probably about 150 feet above my car. It was really odd. It was shaped like a teardrop or a rain drop, but lying on its side.

This was probably midnight or twelve thirty and there was a full moon out behind me with not a cloud in the sky. I had a perfect view of this thing. The round part of this object was facing east, and the tail of it tapered to what looked to be a point to me. The moon was shining on it so I couldn't see the surface, but the very tip of it. It was either a black or a dark grey, something like that. This thing had wings like an airplane, and they were kind of swept back at maybe a forty-five-degree angle. It didn't have a tail section like a regular airplane would, the tail just came to a point. On the leading edge of each wing there were what I kind of thought were windows. There were six or eight round yellow dots that looked like they were illuminated from within. The tip of each wing and on the tip of the front of this thing there looked to be stationary spotlights. They shone down toward the ground, but the lights didn't quite reach.

I left my car with my radio and lights on just to see if it would cause anything to happen to the car. It was fine, but you hear reports of cars sputtering out or radio stations becoming full of static when you see something like this. As this thing went over my car, there was no sound. I watched it go over my car and behind me a bit. I turned around to see what the other two lights were doing, and they were doing their same thing. I turned back to where this object was, and it was totally gone, as though it disappeared.

At the time, I didn't know anything about stealth blimps or that kind of stuff because I was pretty new to this type of thing. I just know that it had wings which I thought were kind of odd. It didn't have a tail section, which was weird, and it didn't make any noise. I didn't know what it was then, and I don't know what it was now. Interestingly enough, west of Columbus is Dayton, which is where Wright-Patterson Air Force Base is located. That is the westerly direction where these things looked like they were coming from.

The thing flew over my car and disappeared. I stood there for a while and searched the horizon from the west, side to side, and couldn't see anything but the stars and the moon. So, I got in my car and drove home. The rest of my way I never saw that third light again. I just saw the other two lights going through their little pattern. Maybe a week or so later, the lights just disappeared and I've never seen them since.

—*Mike, Florida*

67
UFO Validation

I've only once had an experience like this but it is etched in my mind. I was eight or nine-years-old at the time, and my mom had just picked my brother and me up from our grandma's house. We were getting out of the car, with my mother carrying my little brother in a car infant seat.

The sky was a hazy purple and dark, but not pitch black yet. That happens to be my favorite time of the night, so I was looking intently up at the sky. I was admiring the different purple hues, the clouds, and everything. While I was looking up I saw this almost circular, but irregularly shaped object fly across the sky. It wasn't fast like a shooting star, but it was really big. It just moved across the sky and disappeared into the horizon where I couldn't see it anymore.

I was standing there wondering what in the world I had seen. Then, a second one came. They both went left to right from where I was standing. I told my mom about this later and she said, "Danielle, do you not remember me running over to you that night?" I said that I didn't. She added, "For a split second, twice, I couldn't see you, because all I could see was bright light." I told her, "No, I don't remember you running over to me, I just remember getting goosebumps and being like 'that was weird' and going inside." She said, "No, it was so bright I could not see you standing." All this and I was probably twenty feet from her. She said it was just for a split second, but it was just crazy.

I live in New Mexico and I went to Roswell on a trip with my husband to the UFO museum there. I was curious because I had never heard of anybody describing what I had seen. Yes, I knew that other ships had been described by those who have had sightings, but not like what I saw. There they had an exhibit that showed various pictures of objects that have been photographed in the sky over the years, and I found one that matched exactly what I saw. It was just a little picture in a large collage, but that kind of validated it for me. What I remembered happened. It really did.

—*Danielle, New Mexico*

68

Ring Around the UFO

B ack in 2010, I was walking with a friend of mine. It was a nice fall evening. I looked up in the sky and I saw that it was very clear out. I began pointing out constellations and planets in the sky to my friend. All of a sudden, my friend saw a very bright light in the sky and he said, "Is that Venus?" I said, "No, I don't think it's Venus. I don't know what it is. It's probably an airplane." So we just watched it but it was very, very bright. It was like when Venus is unusually bright in the sky and a lot people usually report it as a UFO.

At first, I didn't think it was moving, or it was moving very slowly. Then it started moving a little faster. I don't know if that was because it was getting closer or due to its angle. It started out slower, it stopped, and then it started moving towards us.

It was very strange. It was moving about 1,000, maybe 2,000 feet from the ground. It stopped right above us. We had our necks craned way up, looking at the light in the sky. It was just sitting there for a couple of seconds, and then it got smaller and smaller. Next, it turned blue and red with a ring around it. I think the reason we thought it was getting smaller was that it was going up.

I didn't know what it was. I call it a UFO because it was unidentified to me. I know what airplanes look like. I know a little bit about astronomy and this was something very unusual. It was unexplainable. I was telling my neighbor about this thing I saw in the sky, and she said that she had seen the same thing in the sky when she was a kid three decades ago. She'd lived in our neighborhood that long. Same thing, it came from the north, and was heading south. It stopped above her. Then, it appeared to get smaller, but she thought it didn't go straight up. It turned bluish-red with a ring around it and disappeared. It was in the same city, the same location.

It emitted no sound, no trails or anything behind it, except that strange little ring. It had a smoke ring around it when it went straight up.

Both my friend and I felt it sensed us. I think we both found that strange. I've seen other things and my hunch was that they were man-made, but this was different. It seemed to be not of this planet. I don't know what it was. I did feel that it was intelligent and knew we were looking at it.

There was nothing like missing time in case you wondered. Actually, I had reported it to the National UFO Reporting Center. When I was scrolling through their site I saw that someone just south of me reported something that sounds extremely similar to what we saw.

—*Kirby, Illinois*

PART SIX

UNTIL OUR NEXT CAMPFIRE

A Physician Meets the Supernatural—A Finale

Jim's Note: I like to end each Campfire book with a story that will make you think a bit until we meet again. This one fits the bill.

I qualified as a physician several years ago and since then I've have had two or three quite unusual experiences. The most memorable was one which I really could not put down to just reasonable, rational explanation. It happened several years ago now when I first qualified, and it must have been within the first four months or so of actually starting work. I was on quite a late night shift in one of the hospitals in Wales.

I was downstairs in what is known as the medical admissions unit, just seeing a couple of patients who had been referred in by their family doctor, when I got a cardiac arrest call. Now, when you're on nights, there's a whole team of people and the medical team generally all carry bleepers. You call them beepers in the States. Over the bleepers, I received a cardiac arrest call. I was the most junior member of the team, and because of that, I was doing pretty much the dogsbody kind of work in the medical admissions unit. I was quite far away from where this cardiac arrest call was.

In this particular hospital, we had several wards on either side. It was probably four or five stories tall. The medical admissions unit is on the lower ground floor. The cardiac arrest call that I had was upstairs on the fourth floor, the top floor, of the hospital. So I knew that I was quite far away and that there were members of the team that would be there before me. I had four or five flights of stairs to climb, so I didn't rush because I didn't want to be completely out of breath by the time I actually arrived there. I was running up these stairs and I got to the third floor, which I think in American parlance would be the fourth floor. When I got to the landing area there, I came across a man who was just standing looking out the window. This man was in probably his late sixties, possibly early seventies, and I didn't take that much notice of him because I was in the middle of trying to get to the cardiac arrest call without completely making myself conk out through exertion. Yet, I couldn't help notice that he was naked from the waist down, which was rather unusual. It was something you notice, but again this is a medical ward where we do have elderly patients. Some have dementia and they do go wandering. This was in the middle of the night. Still, it was unusual, and it did make me stop for a second.

I looked at him and he was wearing a mint green t-shirt and nothing else. He wasn't talking or doing anything, but just standing there looking out the window. I didn't stop, but I opened the door of one of the wards and I shouted, "There's a man in the corridor, can you come and get him?" Then I carried on. I had one more of flight of stairs to climb to get to the call. When I arrived on the ward, I went into one of the side rooms where the arrest team was. There was lots of noise, lots of people talking, bustling, and I knew that I was pretty much the last person to arrive, given how far I'd come.

I must have froze when I saw the person who was being worked on in the room, because someone turned around and said to me, "What's the matter, Farbod?" I didn't say anything. I kind of clicked back into reality. Here is the incredible part of the story. The person whose heart had stopped and who was being worked on, was the same man who I had seen on the floor below, looking out the window. I forgot about it in a way and just got on with it to provide assistance, but obviously this affected me.

The man in arrest was naked from the waist down in the bed, and he was wearing a mint green t-shirt. I'm getting goosebumps just talking about it now. We were there for about twenty minutes or so, but the guy very clearly had a very significant episode, and he passed away. As everything was being cleared up and I had considered what I had seen, I thought that if I went back downstairs where I shouted at the nurses to come and collect this half naked person, perhaps they'd tell me, "Oh yes, we found this man." Maybe it was all a big coincidence and for some reason, my mind had played a trick on me. Perhaps I was a little bit hypoxic, having run up the stairs, and my perception had been a bit altered. So I thought I'd go downstairs and speak to the nurses who would confirm that yes, there was an elderly gentleman standing there and they'd put him back to bed and everything was fine.

Of course, when I went downstairs and spoke to the nurses there, they were all chattering because I had frightened them. They hadn't seen anything whatsoever. They'd just heard the door to the stairwell open up and someone shout, "There's a man here."

By the time they managed to check, there was no one there. That just made me feel even more creeped out.

It is relatively difficult to reconcile something like this. Still, I consider medicine as more of an art than a science. The science of it is based a lot on statistics and being able to interpret risks, understanding various aspects of the very hard science of medicine, which would be chemical, physiology, anatomy and things like this. Yet, one thing I have never discounted when treating people in my practice over the years, is the consciousness aspect of medicine, how important it is to cater to people's psychological needs and their spiritual needs, whether you believe or not. It has great power over the well-being of people. You always have to respect it, whether you agree with it or not.

I definitely have moments in my career where someone's spiritual beliefs, or shall we say their faith in the art or the science of medicine has made the medicine work in a way that probably wouldn't be explainable in a statistical or physiological format, but it does work. Everyone knows about the placebo effect and that it makes people feel better. So, I can't discount the power of human consciousness. Whether there is an externalized force or not, I'm not sure. I've seen things like I've explained to you, which makes me think that perhaps there is something beyond the biomechanical workings of the human body.

—*Farbod, United Kingdom*

CLOSING THOUGHTS

Thanks for reading *True Ghost Stories: Jim Harold's Campfire 4*. I appreciate it! I hope that you enjoyed reading it as much as I enjoyed curating these great stories. A special thank you goes out to all of the *Campfire* storytellers.

As for the future, I have many more stories in my emporium of spookiness. Stay tuned for *True Ghost Stories: Jim Harold's Campfire 5* coming in 2016.

If you enjoyed this book, please leave a review on Amazon.com, it helps more than you'll ever know!

If you enjoyed this book and haven't read the others in my Campfire series, here is a link that will take you to my author page at Amazon where you can find (and buy) them all: http://jimharoldbooks.com.

Please tell your friends and family about this book! Don't forget, the ebook of *True Ghost Stories: Jim Harold's Campfire 4* also makes a great gift for less than the cost of a fancy coffee!

Thanks and see you soon.

Stay spooky!

Jim Harold
JimHarold.com
September 2015

AUDIO BONUS/FREE STUFF—CAMPFIRE 4

1. As a special bonus, every buyer of the book gets access to a free audio program featuring my top five favorite stories from this book. These are the original stories as told to me on my podcast, Jim Harold's Campfire. Here is the link to listen to this program created exclusively for readers like you: http://jimharold.com/campfire4bonus.

2. If you enjoyed this book, you will almost certainly want to take a listen to the free, weekly podcast on which it is based. To check it out, go over to http://jimharold.com where you will find *Campfire* and my other free podcasts, *The Paranormal Podcast* and *The Paranormal Report*. The shows are also available on iTunes, and via many other podcast apps.

3. If you'd like to get a weekly batch of paranormal news plus updates on my podcasts and books, please sign up to my free newsletter at jimharold.com/free-newsletter/.

4. Also, check out my free *Jim Harold Central* app for phones and tablets (Apple/iOS, & Android) at http://jimharold.com/apps—the apps are also available on Google Play and the Apple App Store.

Thanks for reading. If this book is our first introduction, I hope this is the start of a beautiful relationship!

Jim

ABOUT THE AUTHOR

Jim Harold is America's most popular paranormal podcast host. With his three free programs, *The Paranormal Podcast*, *Jim Harold's Campfire*, and *The Paranormal Report*, Jim has developed a loyal following that spans the globe.

In 2005, Jim created *The Paranormal Podcast*. After over a decade of working on the business side of media, Jim decided it was time to dust off his broadcast training and step back behind the mic. A life long interest in the paranormal, combined with his love of broadcasting and technology, inspired Jim to create some the most successful podcasts of their type to date. Jim has worked in radio, video, print, and new media.

He holds a Master's Degree in Applied Communication Theory and Methodology and has also taught at the university level.

Jim's free podcasts are regularly among the top podcasts on iTunes in their respective categories and compete with mainstream media publishers such as NPR and many others. Jim lives in Ohio with his fantastic wife, two daughters, and two very rambunctious dogs. He is incredibly thankful for them and his loyal audience. If you want to check out Jim's free podcasts visit http://jimharold.com.

Also, it is highly suggested that you sign up for his free, paranormal newsletter at http://jimharold.com/free-newsletter/.

Check out his free *Jim Harold Central* app for phones and tablets (Apple/iOS & Android) at http://jimharold.com/apps and on the various app stores.

If you have any questions or comments about the book or Jim's programs, contact him personally at jim@jimharold.com.

<<<<>>>>

Made in the USA
Middletown, DE
30 September 2015